CW00376346

What is Your Business Worth?

A Guide to Valuing Your Company

GEOFFREY DALTON

KOGAN PAGE

First published in 1992

Apart from any fair dealing for the purposes of research or private study, or criticism or review, as permitted under the Copyright, Designs and Patents Act, 1988, this publication may only be reproduced, stored or transmitted, in any form or by any means, with the prior permission in writing of the publishers, or in the case of reprographic reproduction in accordance with the terms of licences issued by the Copyright Licensing Agency. Enquiries concerning reproduction outside those terms should be sent to the publishers at the undermentioned address:

Kogan Page Limited
120 Pentonville Road
London N1 9JN

British Library Cataloguing in Publication Data

A CIP record for this book is available from the British Library.

ISBN 0-7494-0809-X

Typeset by The Castlefield Press of Wellingborough, Northants, and printed and bound in Great Britain by Clays Ltd, St Ives plc.

Contents

Acknowledgements

This book could not have been written without a great deal of help and advice from my colleagues at David Garrick and from friends and associates active in the merger and acquisition field.

Detailed comments and advice on the text from Robert Gore, Subhash Thakrar, Nigel Higinbotham and Maureen Wilson-Wright proved invaluable. However, the views expressed and the mistakes made are my own.

Geoffrey Dalton

Chapter 1

Why Bother to Value Your Business?

A finger on the pulse

We all have friends who check the *Financial Times* daily to plot the progress of their stocks and shares. They receive statements from their brokers summarising holdings income and values, and work out whether they are ahead or not this month.

Many of us who are interested in residential property will cast an eye over the local newspaper once a week or check with a friendly estate agent to see what is on the market as an indication of the current value of our own house – our single most important investment perhaps.

Those more concerned with their physical condition will monitor their blood pressure or cholesterol level or find themselves incapable of passing a weighing scale without a quick check.

Staying on top of things is a high priority for many of us. However, there are others who couldn't be less concerned. Some investors buy stocks for a rainy day and put them away for 20 years without once checking the current share price. They may be in for a pleasant surprise, or a nasty shock, when they see the company in receivership.

Equally, we all know of someone who has not been to the doctor for 15 years. He (or she) would be understandably shocked to be told that he has developed a serious illness which, if identified earlier, could have been easily treated.

These are the extremes. I am sure that you and I fall into the sensible middle ground. We cast our eye over stock market values once in a while, take a healthy interest in house prices, and visit our doctor once a year for a check-up. In short, we set up and follow some form of maintenance programme.

Keeping an eye on the family business

But what about the health and current value of your business? This is an important question where that business generates the income and capital necessary to sustain your present standard of living and also provides a personal lifestyle. How about a maintenance programme here? It could be vitally important to value such an asset from time to time – and keep an eye on trends that will affect your future prospects and retirement possibilities.

Unfortunately, it is not easy to make a quick or accurate valuation of a private business in the way that is possible with a quoted stock. I suggest, however, that even a rough valuation can point out some surprising facts and suggest alternative courses of action.

There are occasions, however, when a valuation is absolutely essential.

- If you are thinking of selling your company in the near future it is obviously important to form some idea of its likely value.
- Alternatively, you may be admitting a partner or buying out a director who wishes to retire. In such cases knowing what the business is worth is critical.
- A messy divorce will often focus considerable attention on the current value of the family business, representing, as it probably does, a significant jointly held asset.

But if none of these significant events looms over you and things are jogging along nicely, why bother?

Is the business earning its keep?

If you were the financial director of a public company you would be expected to consider regularly the value of each subsidiary and check the return or service it is providing. You would have shareholders on your back and it would be part of your job to make sure the company's assets are working as hard as possible. In current language, given the increasing competitiveness of business generally, it is necessary to make the assets 'sweat'.

If a subsidiary is not performing to target or has outlived its usefulness or if the funds can be deployed to better effect elsewhere, the directors will consider ways of either improving the operation or disposing of it.

Shouldn't you, as the owner of a business, do the same thing?

The value of the business to you

Well, assuming you are actively employed in the business, there are differences. The income generated is important, of course, in helping you to meet the monthly bills. The fringe benefits and perks for both you and your family also come in useful.

However, that business also offers you a personal lifestyle, an established position and perhaps an absorbing interest that you might find difficult to replace. You might even find yourself unemployable after all these years!

Do not underestimate these values. They are real and important. You may be swimming in a small pond but at least it's *your* pond.

On the other hand, you may feel it is time for a change – a chance to do something different. One million pounds might certainly help to expand your horizons and interests, particularly if you have been scraping along on £35,000 a year and a five-year-old Ford Granada. What is more, if you plan carefully, there may be ways in which you can have your cake and eat it too. This will be discussed later.

Be prepared for an approach

Whatever your situation, at least you should be aware of the possible alternatives and you should review your options from time to time. A word of caution, however. I suggest that the value you put on your business is based on a realistic appraisal of its worth in the current market place and not simply a summation of golf club locker room gossip (inspiration 'from the bottom of the bottle', as one wag put it), pie in the sky numbers generated by a business broker, anxious to lock you in, or over-optimistic values generated by 'good news' specialists.

If you have only a hazy idea of what the business is worth you could become any buyer's lawful prey.

I am constantly amazed at the number of owners who will seriously consider the first offer received for their business, having never really thought about either its value or what capital they would require to replace the income it provides.

Typically, a buyer or business broker contacts you, talks 'telephone numbers' and succeeds in unsettling the whole family. Your eyes glaze over like those of the little old lady in the *Antiques Roadshow* who discovers that her pottery doorstop is really Ming porcelain worth £40,000.

Often the lure of receiving substantial capital for the first time in your life is irresistible and both you and your wife are already thinking in terms of a villa above Cannes, Gucci shoes and a new Mercedes-Benz. Before the money is on the table, in fact, you are already spending it!

Frequently, before you know what is happening, you are psychologically deep into negotiations and will find it difficult to pull out. Worse still, the final offer that emerges after weeks of negotiations with lawyers and accountants often bears no resemblance to the initial proposal.

Your vision of a villa in the South of France has to be abruptly replaced with checking prices of semi-detached houses in Barton-on-Sea. The cash you were putting down as a deposit on your daughter's new home in Surbiton is now badly needed to produce a reasonable retirement income.

The result is that no one in the family is happy and everyone blames you! Do not get caught in that trap.

The pre-emptive strike by an experienced buyer is often astonishingly successful – after all, he's practised it many times.

If, in contrast, you have formed a reasonable idea of the value of your business, this will enable you to sidestep such a 'play' and give you time to plan ahead. If you do receive a superlative offer it will also enable you to recognise it for what it is, accept it eagerly, and lock in the buyer decisively and quickly before he can change his mind.

Questions to ask yourself

There are other advantages to considering, at least occasionally, the market value of your business and certainly a number of questions you should ask yourself:

1. Am I getting a reasonable return on my investment?

Here we are talking about a return related to the current value, not the historical cost, and you are acting, in fact, as your own financial director.

About three years ago, working on behalf of a large European buyer, we offered £3.5 million to the shareholders of a distribution company with net tangible assets of about that amount. The shares were held by 40 members of the family scattered across the western hemisphere who had delegated management responsibility to a comfortable and satisfied management team.

After satisfying the needs of that team, the family received a total dividend of £40,000 a year, representing a 1 per cent return on their investment. In short, they were forgoing, perhaps, £300,000–£400,000 a year of income which they could have earned on, say, gilts.

This sacrifice might have been reasonable if the company was really going places, expanding rapidly, ploughing back earnings into new equipment and new developments. In fact, the business, blessed with unimaginative management, was steadily losing market share and accumulating unsaleable inventory.

For largely emotional reasons, I suspect, the shareholders rebuffed our offer. They must now be regretting it. In the current market they would find it difficult to raise even £1 million for the business.

2. Would the capital released by a sale be sufficient to enable me to do the things I've always wanted to do?

This triggers a whole range of questions from capital gains tax payable on the proceeds, income anticipated from capital investments and other sources of income, to the type of plans you have made for the future.

If your children have flown the nest and your ongoing financial responsibilities have declined, in most cases your needs for income will diminish considerably – despite what your life insurance salesman might argue!

If, on the other hand, you have always hankered to go into international power boat racing or wish to start a new business or travel the world extensively, the calculation will be more difficult.

Whatever your plans may be, test them for realism. Do not make the mistake of assuming, even after all these years of effort, that the world owes you a living.

3. Will the value of my business be affected by my personal role?

If you put in only occasional attendance, restricting your role to supplying new initiatives or limiting your participation to 'touches at the tiller', this will certainly help to boost the value of the business – all other things being equal. If you can be away for lengthy periods, acting in effect as a chairman figure, this is something a buyer will appreciate and value.

If, however, you have to be in there at 8 o'clock on Monday morning to open up and the employees are dependent on you for day-to-day operating decisions, do you really have anything to sell beyond your own personal services?

If your role falls into the second category, you had better start delegating and training right now. If you want anything to sell you must learn to trust others, let them take decisions, give them their heads and provide substantial financial incentives for them to become involved.

Better to have 80 per cent of the cake than 100 per cent of nothing!

4. Am I taking too much out of the business and will this reduce its future value?

If you, or your family, are taking out excessive salaries or benefits this will impact not only on the apparent profitability of the business but will also drain away cash and essential working capital.

A successful, expanding business will literally gobble up cash in high growth years and you cannot expect the bank to finance this expansion 100 per cent. Even if the bank is prepared to do so, their support may come at a very high cost both in terms of interest and servicing charges and may also put you at their mercy in the form of loans repayable on demand.

In my experience, far too many businesses are being asked to support unrealistically high lifestyles, often with disastrous consequences. Owning your own company is not an automatic entitlement to driving a £50,000 car, or borrowing to buy a small country estate, or spending 15 to 20 hours a week at the golf club!

Older generations cite the impact of 98 per cent tax rates to defend such practices. 'Thirty somethings' argue that they have to keep up with their friends – the Joneses!

Either way, if the business is being asked to support an unrealistic burden, the chances of reaping a respectable selling price are very much reduced.

5. Could I improve the value of the business significantly by investing more money or time in it?

This is not an easy question to answer. Many business people, responding to Thatcherite exhortations to invest in the mid-1980s, have bitterly regretted their actions, as consumer and business confidence collapsed and market demand evaporated. This left them, in many cases, with heavy bank debt that still had to be paid back.

In some ways, this is the corollary to the previous question, except that here we are talking of purchasing new equipment, developing new marketing programmes or investing in management training, rather than simply building cash and working capital.

It is equally difficult to decide to invest more time in the business. Time spent training others to take over must be a good investment. With your knowledge of the market place, products and services, efforts to build sounder business plans must also be of value. Continuing to carry on with mundane, run of the mill, clerical operations cannot be the right way to spend your time and will not improve the value of your business.

Value perceptions

We have asked a number of questions in the previous paragraphs which relate to the real underlying value of the business. But what about the presentation of results?

With a little foresight, you could ask an accountant, who does not know the business well, for an informal valuation. He comes back with some numbers and you are disappointed at the value he suggests. In his defence he points out that the company reported only £40,000 profit last year.

You respond, impatiently, that you, your wife, Aunt Sally and other members of the family have extracted £160,000 from the business in one form or another during the same period. It has to be worth more than that!

Unfortunately, by burying these benefits in the accounts to keep them safe from prying eyes you may have made it difficult to value the business at anything like its true worth.

The buyer will make an offer on perceived values and accordingly it may be difficult for you to substantiate the true earnings of the company.

In a case like this, you should consider allowing those benefits to surface over a few years. Provide Aunt Harriet with a dividend each year, for instance, instead of a salary and a car. Pay for holidays out of your own pocket rather than charging to the company all those abortive sales missions to Australia and New Zealand. Be prepared to take your medicine for two or three years if you are intent on building up the value of the business.

In 1987 I received the prospectus of a financial services company seeking to raise capital for acquisitions and expansion. It was a great time to seduce the investor – a few months before the crash! On a slight increase in turnover over the previous year, the accountants had produced annual profits which soared from £10,000 to £400,000.

On studying the situation further I realised that the key employees/shareholders had simply converted 90 per cent of their remuneration into dividends to help things along. They had also generously agreed to buy back their company cars and assume personal responsibility for the associated running costs.

The result of these and other cosmetic adjustments was to create a healthy pretax profit, on the back of which the public promptly invested £1.5 million for a small stake. Needless to say, following this investment, the company has not continued to progress at quite the same rate.

Who said the age of miracles has passed? In the merger and acquisition trade this is an extreme example of a company being 'groomed for sale'.

I do not want to suggest for a moment that you engage in such skulduggery, but I recommend that you make an honest attempt to allow the genuine earnings attractions to show through.

Summary

Why not make a serious attempt to value your business every two or three years?

As part of the exercise, ask yourself:

1. *After receiving reasonable remuneration for my time and effort, am I getting an adequate return also for my investment, taking into account the inherent level of risk in this business?*

If prime bank rates are at 12 per cent, you need at least 15–20 per cent per annum on the current value of your equity investment over and above your salary.

2. *Is the business likely to provide me with enough capital or income to retire on, or must I look for other sources of support for my old age?*

Remember your needs and expenses are going to decline after 65.

3. *How dependent is the business on my personal efforts? Can I lessen this dependence? Are there others around who could achieve significant improvements if I gave them their head and provided them with more incentive?*

Successful delegation will almost invariably improve the value of your business in the eyes of a buyer.

4. Am I or is my family making unrealistic demands on the business in terms of remuneration or benefits? Am I sure that all costs are wholly, necessarily and exclusively incurred for the business?

Restraint now could dramatically improve the capital value in a few years' time by allowing the real earning potential to show through. A business strapped for cash will rarely command the best price.

5. Should I invest more money and/or time into the business to improve its worth? Perhaps I should invest in new equipment, marketing or staff training? Would improvements here make a significant difference?

Answering these points raises the obvious questions, including amount of investment involved, probable rate of return, risk factors and availability and cost of funds.

- Will the investment made actually improve the value of the company after the borrowings are taken into account?
- Will profits flow through before probable date of sale?

These are difficult questions to answer with honesty, and tough hurdles to surmount. But focusing on such basics is certainly the place to start. Making even a rough initial valuation will certainly stimulate this type of thinking.

Chapter 2

Why This Book was Written

Introduction

Over the years I have met many owners who are intent on selling their businesses. They are impressive people in their own fields, experts perhaps in managing engineering companies, clothing distributors, commodity traders, or whatever.

They may have devoted every waking hour to the business and it has assumed an almost human role as far as they are concerned. Success has often been achieved at the cost of a divorce, the alienation of children and the consumption of all the owner's energies, leaving no time for other interests or pastimes.

Without doubt, they have had to battle with the Inland Revenue, the VAT inspector, employer's liability problems and so on, apart from the endless and predictable wrestling that goes on with suppliers and customers in an increasingly competitive market place.

They will have burnt the midnight oil, travelled over weekends, mortgaged the family home up to the hilt and lived for years on a financial knife edge.

No wonder most owners have only enough energy to build one business! Creating and growing even one business in a lifetime is still a significant achievement.

In many cases, the entrepreneur will have started in business on leaving school at 16 and will never have gone on to higher education. Statistically, relatively few successful entrepreneurs have university degrees.

We are all familiar with the old story of the successful market trader who sells everything for double his purchase price and then claims he is satisfied with a 5 per cent gross margin!

Often the impressions the owner has of the value of his business have been derived from chats with friends at the golf club or, more likely, the pub, or from information gleaned on deals done and reported in the *Daily Telegraph*. He may know competitors who have sold out. Some may have done very well, and will proudly broadcast their success; there will be many others who have bitterly regretted selling and felt out-smarted.

Is it any wonder that when an offer comes right out of the blue it catches the owner completely unprepared? Initially, the offer may seem attractive and he does not need a calculator to work out that interest on the amount offered at 10 per cent per annum will give him a very acceptable lifestyle for the rest of his days. The buyer's soothing assurances will often do the rest.

The owner/manager is often lonely. It is the one comment that I hear time and again in talking to such people. If he is still married he may not discuss the business in any detail with his wife. For one thing he doesn't want to worry her with the risks he is taking and the inherent volatility in trading that he sees from day to day.

He is used to making all the decisions himself and may never have developed good delegation skills. After all, over the years he has only had himself to satisfy. He has become, of necessity, self-reliant and fairly autocratic. He has had no real boss other than the customers and suppliers with whom he deals. As a result he may have developed an idiosyncratic style of management. In many cases, he will not have encouraged any meaningful business dialogue with his employees.

Although he may know all there is to know about the design, manufacture and marketing of infra-red heating systems, he will be completely out of his depth in trying to value or sell his business.

Who can he turn to for objective advice?

Sources of advice

The accountant

He may talk things over with his accountant, typically a small provincial firm which has supported him through thick and thin over the years with accounting services and general business advice.

The accountancy firm predictably offers a range of financially related skills, including audit work, personal and corporate tax advice, insurance, corporate secretarial support etc. However, often the accountant will be out of his depth when advising on the valuation and sale of the business. It is not something he is asked to do very often.

Most accountants are not pro-active in any case, and may well have chosen that career as one suited to their natural predispositions to check, balance and record.

Where the accountant does give advice it may be influenced by reported profits, personal tax considerations, historical costs and book values. It may well be a case of familiarity breeding contempt.

Having grown up with a business over many years and recognising it 'warts and all', the accountant may simply not be able to bring objectivity to bear. He will hate to admit that he cannot help, however, and is certainly not going to refer a lifelong client to one of the major city firms. He inevitably has a problem since, if the business is sold, he will probably lose the annual audit and it may be one of his 'bread and butter' clients.

The solicitor

When approached with this problem, the family solicitor will exude confidence and view it as just another conveyancing assignment. To him there is little difference between selling a business and selling property. He will concern himself immediately with the problems posed by warranties, guarantees, undertakings and so on and will regard these as the key issues. One city solicitor even admitted this to me recently, suggesting that the warranties were, of course, the essential 'meat' of the forthcoming negotiations!

Solicitors are highly literate but much less comfortable with figures. Some have difficulty in getting the right number of zeros behind the pound signs in the final sales contract! Many use, and hide behind, a seemingly standard and ubiquitous word-processed sales contract that seems to pop up all across the country, seeing the whole exercise as essentially one of filling in blanks and deleting inappropriate sections.

I have also encountered solicitors who sprinkle around business valuations like confetti! In some cases, their relationship to the client is so strong that he will treat their opinion as one of the Ten Commandments – frequently with disastrous results!

The banker

Our businessman can, of course, talk to his old friend the local banker, assuming there is one left in the country who has been in the job for more than a few months! In truth, the role of the banker is a rapidly changing one and commercial pressures are reducing him to a somewhat robot-like existence. In any case, the typical banker is so mesmerised by security or break-up values that it is difficult for him to give objective advice.

The seminar

Our owner could go to a seminar and share the lecturer's wisdom and pronouncements with 150 other participants at £350 a time. These seminars, however, tend to be pitched primarily at the corporate finance executive and it is necessary to learn and understand a new language first. To retain their hold on the market most professionals are going to do nothing to demystify the whole merger and acquisition process.

There are, of course, smaller seminars conducted around the country where it is possible to absorb some practical information in five or six hours.

Books

Another approach is to buy a book on the subject. I set out to do this and found that it was a frustrating exercise. Some of the books I picked up were impressive, learned works of professional excellence, suitable for detailed reference from time to time by those seeking an answer to specific share valuation or merger and acquisition problems. These books, however, tend to be written for the professional and are too technical for the equipment manufacturer from Croydon.

Alternatively, some of the literature is so bland and idealistic that it reminded me of old British Rail travel posters showing the family on summer holiday in Ilfracombe – a nice colourful picture, nothing specifically wrong, but not how it really is once you are there! In addition, £35 seems an awful lot to pay for pretty pictures!

There seemed to be nothing available for the type of owner whom I have met during my business career – in other words, a book that is easily readable, contains practical advice and describes specific illustrative situations that the author has personally encountered. There seemed to be a need for a book emphasising everyday problems rather than one highlighting those technical anomalies and curiosities that are so fascinating to the professional adviser.

You sell only once

The probability is that you, as a business owner, are going to sell only once. In consequence, you are not going to get the chance to refine your business selling skills and those skills you learned marketing heating systems may not be helpful.

What makes matters even worse is that you may be up against a professional buyer or buying team. Many public companies have assembled formidable merger and acquisition teams who have probably bought six businesses already this year. Their pace, systematic approach, assurance, presentation and, indeed, bonhomie are awe-inspiring. For them this is just another day and just another deal.

For you, in contrast, it may be the end of an era; the end of a 20-year love affair. In your eyes, there is more to valuing and selling your business than cash flows, profit projections, warranties and loan stock. It is an emotional parting of the ways. It may also be your one chance to ensure that you will never be in financial need again.

And yet it is all happening so fast. You have never really had a chance to think about the value of the business before, or considered fully what it means to you and your family. It is all very upsetting. Almost before you have accepted the idea of selling and recognised the implications, you are being asked to take buyers round the factory and find yourself introducing them to your friends and colleagues. By then it is all too late; the clock is starting to run.

The unequal contest

You will have realised by now that I am convinced there is all too often complete inequality in bargaining power between buyer and seller in such situations. It is my hope that by reading through this book you will develop a feel for valuing your business and getting into the right frame of mind regarding its possible sale. It should also help to focus your thoughts on the implications and ramifications of selling or entering into discussions with that possible objective.

Being aware of how the buyer might value your business, being able to anticipate his questions and foreseeing the reasons he will cite for reducing his offer will help you to develop the counter arguments and strategy necessary to ensure that it is a more balanced contest.

I will also suggest where you can obtain impartial, disinterested advice and provide you with some ways of checking on the quality and objectivity of that advice.

Chapter 3

Vendor Beware!

Introduction

You may have inherited the business or have founded your own company and nurtured it over the years to its present rude health. You may well have become an expert on mechanical handling systems, plumbing materials, dyestuffs, tropical fish or some other area of economic activity. It is unlikely, however, that you have actively bought and sold businesses for a living or have had much experience in valuing them.

In succumbing to an unsolicited approach from a buyer and, perhaps, by implication accepting his valuation of your company, you may be diving head first into shark-infested waters. It is difficult to escape from such an experience in one piece unless you use effective shark repellent! A sound valuation can certainly improve the odds of emerging unscathed.

It is worthwhile describing the negotiation process first in all its gory detail.

A cautionary tale

Many years ago, we received a call from a lady seeking our advice. Her husband, who had recently died, had founded a company which manufactured electronic components. It was a company with considerable innovative skills, selling high quality products to demanding customers. Her husband had had the foresight to put his shares into an offshore 'freezer' trust as a tax planning and minimisation device. Unfortunately, he had 'shuffled off this mortal coil' without any prior warning to family or employees.

A few days after the funeral, the widow was telephoned by a Jersey solicitor to say that the trustees had received an offer from the management of the company of £1,250,000 for the business. The trustees recommended prompt acceptance of this offer and suggested reinvestment of the proceeds in government securities to safeguard the capital and, incidentally, to lighten their own responsibilities. They were understandably concerned at the implications of the widow acting as chairman of a company in which she had had no real technical knowledge or involvement.

Using her intuition, the widow felt that the offer might have been low and sought our advice as to the current value of the business. Having reviewed the most recent financial statements and visited the company premises, we hazarded an initial opinion that the company was worth at least £2 million and suggested that she should not accept the first offer received.

Fortified by this advice, the lady, who was fairly strong willed, persuaded the trustees to ask us to conduct a formal valuation of the business, which we duly did.

This confirmed our initial impressions and put a somewhat higher price range on the business. The trustees expressed incredulity that the company could be worth over £2 million but, as a result of continuing pressure from the widow, agreed to give us a mandate to sell.

Within a few weeks, and after a few lucky breaks, we succeeded in negotiating an offer at the top end of the valuation range from a trade buyer of unquestioned financial strength. This offer was promptly relayed to the trustees.

After a short delay we were informed by the trustees that the management group had increased their offer to exactly the same amount. The trustees now suggested that since the management had initiated the bidding the company should be sold to them.

We disagreed with this proposal, without being so churlish as to ask how they were able to place such a precise valuation on the company, and suggested that both would-be buyers be invited to submit revised offers. The contest thereafter became heated, leading to writs and injunctions and with lawyers on both sides issuing dark threats of retribution etc.

The trustees were caught uncomfortably in the cross-fire and it was obviously not an experience that they relished.

At the end of the day, however, the trust did receive the full proceeds of the sale, something like twice the original amount offered. The blow-by-blow details of the deal would fill a book, but then that is another story.

In this case, we were lucky that the widow had willpower and was prepared to use it. The story also underlines the need for an owner to make sensible provisions during his lifetime to save his partner the trauma of selling the business at a difficult time.

The buyer's ploys

Thrusting managements in a few dozen public companies, enjoying sky-high share multiples, had a field day in the 1980s picking up smaller businesses like ripe cherries. They assembled teams of negotiators and accounting and legal advisers who chose to hunt in packs.

This proved an effective formula and many an unsuspecting owner was seduced into selling his company by the aid of smooth, persuasive presentations and seemingly irresistible logic. It had almost reached the stage that 'if this is Tuesday, this must be the Croydon Widget Company'.

Many of these acquisitions were profitable for the buyers. You do not need a computer to work out that offering your shares, enjoying perhaps a 20 times earnings multiple, to purchase the assets of a private company at, say, a 5 times multiple, does wonders for your trading results and capital values.

Although this torrid pace has now slackened and, indeed, many hunting packs have been disbanded, there are still plenty of professional buying teams around. As mentioned earlier, this creates unequal negotiating strength between buyer and seller. Perhaps it is worth documenting the basic strategy adopted by some of the more aggressive acquisition teams.

Lighting the fuse

Initially, they will tempt you with a once-in-a-lifetime opportunity to sell your company for an enormous price. The techniques they use are much in evidence on Saturday mornings at your local market or among the traders on the seaside pier.

They make an offer you cannot sensibly refuse and suggest that you simply sit back while they do all the work. They exude confidence and geniality and subtly play on enhancing your self-image. You are encouraged to think of how you can place or spend the money – an absorbing exercise for most of us.

Once you are hooked and well and truly into the process, they require additional information. This leads to vociferous demands for detailed information on markets, pricing, costings, products and so on, and develops into requests for aged analyses, supplier analyses, customer analyses, projected results, personnel details, introductions to major customers and suppliers etc.

It obviously becomes necessary for them during this process to meet your key employees. Before you know where you are, your whole team is dedicated to producing reams of information in connection with the sale and all this information has to be checked and cross-checked.

Soon you start to accept the fact that the sale is all over bar the shouting. Your employees start to realign their loyalties and the buyer's team will not be slow in painting a picture of the expanded opportunities available to them as part of a larger dynamic group.

At this point, when everyone is aboard, the squeeze on you starts. The buying team did not apparently realise that there was so much slow-moving stock; they discover a number of doubtful debts; they worry about the quality of the work in progress and recognise belatedly the need to invest considerable capital to expand and put the company on to a truly viable basis. Of course, you may not have access to such capital and that may be one of the reasons why you have decided to sell. And to think you never realised!

They are worried about your lack of computerisation and

point out your vulnerability to supplier pressures; why didn't you recognise this before? They assess your competitors as extremely formidable and through careful analysis have detected small but significant price and profit margin erosions etc.

At the end of this performance you are beginning to convince yourself that they are doing you a favour taking the company off your hands.

It then logically follows that they cannot, in deference to their own shareholders, follow through on their original offer for the company. In view of all the problems and skeletons in the cupboard that they have found, the original offer has to be substantially modified.

At this stage you are exhausted, your staff loyalties are divided, and your sales drive has ground to a standstill for the simple reason that there are no longer any staff left to service the customers properly. Lawyers' and accountants' fees are escalating alarmingly and all in all you scarcely feel like battling on. How did things come to this pass?

Although you never had a clear concept of the value of your business in the first place, you can now see that the original offer was really 'over the top'. You rationalised that the initial offer was so good that you did not want to disturb or discourage the buyer in any way and certainly did not want to upset him by making approaches to other possible buyers or challenging his assumptions. You allowed it to become a one-horse race.

Divided loyalties – the advisers' field day

It is difficult to know who your real allies are, since the loyalties of your advisers quickly become divided.

We have already considered in the previous chapter the difficulty of obtaining good professional advice. For many advisers your company may be a substantial client which the adviser is loath to lose. Moreover, unless you employ one of the larger city firms of accountants or solicitors, they may not be familiar with the valuation and sale of companies.

In consequence, your advisers slow the pace of negotiations

down, double-check everything and spend hours and hours boning up, at your expense, on every aspect of the transaction so that they can keep pace with the buyer's experienced representatives.

For the buyer and his advisers, this is all in a day's work and they are going through a well-rehearsed countdown procedure. However, for your solicitors and accountants, this is a demanding and time-consuming exercise and, whether the deal goes ahead or not, the client, that is *you*, is going to be saddled with some heavy bills.

The buyer insists that you prepare and sign off full audited accounts for the year just ended and your auditors recognise that, for once, their detailed working papers had better be in apple pie order. They check their professional liability insurance cover nervously, redouble their efforts to get everything right and, of course, the costs of this exercise are again charged against you – the hapless vendor.

The distractive index

If, at this late stage, you find that the emerging shape of the final offer is unacceptable, you will have incurred substantial professional costs, expended a tremendous amount of nervous energy, and will hardly be able to face all those employees who treated the transaction as virtually a *fait accompli*. This is apart from the reaction on the home front where your family were expecting a handsome windfall.

Worse still, the business may be suffering through neglect owing to the onerous requirements of this process. This is what we call the distractive index. You need a long holiday to get over it but at this point you just cannot afford to take the time off.

This may be a discouraging scenario but it is not that unusual.

As advisers, we have suffered through this process ourselves. Lots of negotiations do not result in a completed transaction.

The knock-out punch

We know of one international group, active in chasing private company acquisitions in the UK, which has refined these buying techniques to a fine art. They are careful, for instance, to use internal advisers for the bulk of the work; they are certainly not going to pay out £150–£200 an hour to outside solicitors and accountants. They want total control over that element of the acquisition process.

Inevitably, after reams of information have been requested and prepared, and a nerve-racking delay while the buyer does sums and draws conclusions, you are invited to a West End boardroom to receive a formal offer.

Following an obsequiously offered cup of tea or coffee, you are treated to a detailed financial analysis of the acquisition opportunity from the buyer's point of view. Using hi-tech blackboard, overhead slides and computer displays, the buyer will demonstrate in convincing fashion that although an initial offer of £4 million was made, having analysed the situation carefully, such a transaction cannot be financed at a penny more than £2.2 million; your comments are then invited.

Even if you are extremely numerate and articulate and represent yourself well against such professionals, in the long run it inevitably boils down to judgement, ie the buyer's judgement. You can sidestep this 'play' by making it very clear at the outset that no offer below £4 million will be considered.

Beware of easy answers

A friend tells you he sold his business for a price based on six times the pretax earnings. That was a fair price, he claims, Why not use the same multiple for your business?

There is in truth no easy answer. A glance at the price-earnings multiples of quoted companies in the *Financial Times* reveals a range from, say, 2 to 50 times earnings. If that is close enough for you then you can safely put this book away unread. If you would like to get a little more precise, read on.

During the 1980s most small to medium-sized businesses probably sold for between four and seven times pretax earnings. Recession has seen some weakening of these multiples but there are so many variables that it is impossible to generalise. What profits are you using, for instance – historic, current or projected? Are you using reported profits or figures adjusted to reflect the real performance of the business? There can be a world of difference, as we shall see. What about asset cover – particularly where the assets are readily realisable? What about the attractiveness of your business to a particular buyer?

We saw one business recently purchased for 26 times earnings because the buyer, a European group, was determined to get a foothold in a particular UK market sector.

To illustrate, calculate the value of your business at, say, three times pretax profits and, say, five times profits. For most of us it will make a very big difference.

Conclusion

You may think that pitfalls in the process have been exaggerated and buyers credited with almost demonic persistence and greed.

I emphasise from my own experience, however, that this type of conduct is not at all unusual and I suggest that you certainly take the possibility of such behaviour into account.

When you emerge from such an abortive and draining mission you conclude that there has to be a better way. There is – and it starts with deciding your own objectives and priorities. These must include:

- establishing both a target and an acceptable minimum price;
- defining the form and timing of consideration that you are prepared to consider;
- deciding your willingness to remain involved afterwards;
- deciding on assets not to be included in any sale.

All these points should form part of what we, perhaps loosely, call the 'valuation'.

Chapter 4

The Valuation We are Seeking

Introduction

It is as well at the outset to define the type of valuation we are seeking and to differentiate between this valuation and those carried out for other purposes.

Current market value

We will attempt to establish the current market value of the business, ie the price that a buyer will pay to take over your business and possibly enjoy all the fruits and benefits of its activities into the future. This will include use, if not owner-ship, of all the assets essential to the effective running of the business, including the name and goodwill.

If the property is to be retained by the vendor, and if it is essential for the conduct of the business, an arm's-length lease for an acceptable future period will be assumed. We are valuing a business, essentially an income generating system, not just a collection of plant and machinery. Let us consider this further.

At this stage, we are talking about the whole business, ie 100 per cent of the shares, all the assets and all the liabilities, both actual and contingent, pertaining to the business. We are not wrestling with the ramifications of minority interests or the value of a particular class of shares. Our valuation, however, will reflect both the direct liabilities of the business and also those liabilities entered into by the owner personally in connection with the business.

You may have given a charge on your house to secure the bank loan or overdraft, or the bank may have insisted on a personal guarantee. Although these are personal liabilities and do not feature in the audited accounts of the company, they must be taken into account unless, of course, you are prepared to enter into a potentially onerous commitment to continue to provide such guarantees after the sale. This is very unlikely.

We will treat all amounts due to and from the owners, shareholders or parent company as equity for the purpose of our valuation, and where non-business assets are to be excluded from the sale this must be made clear at the outset.

The value of a business is independent of the form of ownership involved. Today, almost all businesses of any size are incorporated as limited companies although some professional associations still require their members to operate as sole traders or in partnerships. Throughout this book I have assumed, unless it is specifically stipulated otherwise, that we are dealing with limited companies.

The predictable buyer

We are seeking the price that would be paid by a predictable buyer, probably a trade buyer, ie someone who knows the industry well and may even know and trade with your company. We are not talking primarily of the opportunistic buyer – someone looking for a 'bargain basement' purchase. Equally, at this stage, we are not taking into account the price that might be paid by a 'premium buyer' or, as we term him, a 'jigsaw player'.

A jigsaw player is a buyer who is assembling perhaps a national chain of stores and finds that you have one of the pieces he is missing. He may have, for example, distribution outlets all over the UK with the exception of South Wales and you have a nice distribution business based in Cardiff. You would ideally wish to sell to such a buyer because he can often offer the best price. It would be wrong, however, to value the company on that basis because there is no certainty that such a buyer can be found.

Professional presentation

The valuation or price we are seeking would only be realised after reasonable efforts have been made to market the business. We will assume that an effective but discreet promotional programme has been undertaken to uncover suitable buyers over a reasonable period of time – typically, two to three months or possibly more.

Timing

We are valuing the business at an agreed point. This could be at year-end or any other convenient date agreed upon. It may be necessary to pro rata profits and estimate taxes for the period from the company's year-end to date of sale.

The value chosen will also assume a sensible and mutually acceptable handover period appropriate to the complexity of or know-how in the business, or in accordance with the reasonable stipulations of the buyer. Some buyers may wish to take over responsibility for running things immediately. This is more likely if they know the business well and are prepared to manage it directly themselves. In other cases, the buyer will insist on the present owners and management team remaining with the business for, say, 12 to 18 months.

If the vendor is unwilling to stay on for a reasonable handover period this may affect the valuation and price that the buyer is willing to pay.

Cash or cash equivalent

We are establishing a valuation based on a purchase price in cash or its equivalent. This consideration can take various forms such as the purchase of equity, the assumption of loans or guarantees, undertakings to make agreed pension contributions, post-acquisition consulting fees, salaries etc.

It may also take the form of shares in the acquiring company. Part may be deferred, and this amount may be defined at completion or be dependent on the future performance of the company. For our valuation to have any real meaning it must express these future and, in some cases, potential benefits as a net present cash value.

We will look in more detail at the different forms of consideration in a later chapter.

Selling under pressure

We are also assuming that there is no undue pressure on the vendor to sell and that the transaction can be completed over a reasonable period. Where the owners are ill or have pressing personal debts which make it imperative to sell the business quickly, these facts will tend to depress the value achievable. This will also be the case if the business itself is in financial difficulty.

If the buyer gets to know of these problems, and the chances are that he will, he will not hesitate to use the information for his own benefit.

Formal valuations

1. Shareholdings

Accountants are often required to value specific shares, classes of shares or shareholdings within a company.

In this case, they are concerned not only with the value of the business as a whole, which may indeed be incidental, but with the inter-relationships between different classes of shares, including rights to dividends, preferential repayments of capital, conversion into other classes of shares etc and with the value or nuisance value of minority holdings.

The rules or practices governing such valuations may be prescribed in the Memorandum and Articles of Association of the company, shareholder agreements or established by precedent set in the courts.

Where your company has a complicated share structure, dissident minority holdings or similar complications, any valuation of a particular shareholding, for instance, will be the subject of different calculation methods.

We are all aware of derisory valuations for minority shareholdings even in profitable companies, where the controlling shareholders pay no dividends and may be dismissive of the rights or entitlements of the minority shareholders. In such a case, 10 per cent of the equity of the company may be virtually unsaleable if it provides neither income to the shareholder nor the prospect of capital realisation.

2. Valuations for tax purposes

The Inland Revenue have a specialised Share Valuation Division dedicated to valuing shares for fiscal or taxation purposes. The need for a valuation may arise, for instance, where control of a company is being transferred overseas. This is essentially a valuation for taxation purposes which may bear little or no relationship to the company's open market value.

Again, valuations for tax purposes will be made following the death of a shareholder.

3. Companies purchasing own shares

Valuations will be made where a company intends to purchase its own shares – a procedure allowed under a change in the Companies Act Rules of 1985. This is essentially a valuation affecting the rights and inter-relationships of the shareholders and is not a valuation necessarily of the whole business at current market values.

Informal valuations

In addition to formal valuations of shares or shareholdings, there are other informal valuations that will be carried out by other interested parties.

1. Banks

Your bank manager is valuing businesses every day for security purposes, ie as cover for the bank loans he is extending. He must take a conservative view – after all he is not in the risk business, officially at least. He would consider he gets little of the 'upside' or profits – apart from his 4 per cent spread, that is. Therefore, he must control carefully the risks that the bank takes.

Bankers can, of course, be over-zealous in their valuations, reciting '25 per cent on stock and work in progress, 40 per cent on debtors etc', as though they were reciting a rosary or chanting a mantra.

Banks will often commission insolvency reports prior to appointing administrators or receivers where a business is in financial trouble. I have seen valuations of inventories at a fraction of their original cost. Debtors may be marked down by 50 per cent, particularly where there may be no ongoing service available in the event of a liquidation. Buildings used by the business are suddenly less valuable, since a new tenant or purchaser must be found in what can be a soft property market. At present, for instance, there seems to be a glut of commercial property available. Hence, often the value of a business on a break-up basis is a fraction of its value as an operating entity.

2. Suppliers

Suppliers or large creditors to your business will often conduct informal valuations for their own purposes to make sure you can pay for all the orders you are placing.

Their views will, of course, be influenced by the profitability and value of your business to them and the level of credit they are extending, both in absolute terms and also relative to your own net worth. If you are a major customer they may, in effect, have a large investment in your business.

Increasingly, overseas suppliers are looking for guarantees to support their lending, particularly to UK retailers, who have not had the best reputation of late.

Summary

Our objective is to reach a fair open market value of your business at an agreed date and on the basis of its sale to a predictable buyer. You may locate a 'jigsaw player' who will pay a large premium for your business when you come to sell but we must not assume, at this stage, that we can sell to such a buyer.

We assume that the business will be properly presented, professionally handled, sold without undue pressure and under reasonable warranties and conditions for immediate cash.

It is, however, to be sold 'warts and all' with adjustments made for any property to be excluded, onerous obligations or contingent liabilities assumed. Questions affecting the business's basic ongoing viability, confused books of account, or inability to substantiate assets, liabilities, costs, revenues or profits will all be reflected in the valuation achieved.

If, however, you are seeking a valuation of a particular shareholding, perhaps because of a shareholder dispute or death or because of the need to establish a potential tax liability, you will not find the answers to these questions in this book.

Satisfying the tax inspector, for example, as to the value of your company is quite different from satisfying a trade buyer.

Chapter 5

The Basic Approach

The predictable buyer

Beauty is in the eye of the beholder. The key to valuing a business is to look at it from the buyer's point of view and to evaluate the particular benefits and advantages that he can derive from the acquisition of your company.

Where you already have a specific buyer in mind, a valuation can be drawn up tailor-made for that situation. This is a one-off valuation, however, which may be difficult to justify if, for any reason, that buyer either loses interest or is unable to complete.

It is much more usual to value the business on the basis of a predictable trade buyer. In this way the valuation developed will have relevance for a wide range of suitors and therefore much more general applicability. Under normal circumstances, the trade buyer will be able to offer you a better price than the individual investor simply seeking an alternative to gilts or other similar investments.

Earnings – will it wash its face?

Since most acquiring companies are seeking to buy earnings, an initial range of values should be calculated based on a multiple of the current and expected earnings of your business. This multiple, in turn, will be related to the profit expectations in that trade sector. Multiples used will reflect other factors impacting on performance, including general levels of interest rates representing, as these do, the cost of borrowings to a buyer, competition and so on.

Many buyers will expect an acquisition to be largely self-financing. In other words, the cash generated by the new business must be sufficient to service the bank debt incurred to finance its purchase. Therefore, this becomes one of the bench-marks we must consider. In trade terms a company passing this test is at least 'washing its face'.

Quoted companies will also be wary of acquisitions which dilute or water down their own earnings per share. This can happen where the return anticipated from the acquisition, relative to the purchase price, is less than the return generated by the parent company in its basic business.

Asset cover

In addition to earnings, a typical buyer will seek support for his investment in the form of assets acquired or 'asset cover'. The buyer likes to feel, if possible, that the bulk of his investment is supported by real and tangible assets acquired, hence the emphasis on valuations based on assets.

Not only does he want the comfort of acquiring bricks and mortar and other tangible assets in exchange for his cash or shares, but any shortfall, termed 'goodwill', has to be written off against retained earnings or revenue reserves. Since this may restrict future dividends that can be paid out, large amounts of goodwill are not popular with shareholders.

Intangibles

In addition to these two traditional methods of valuing a business, we must consider intangibles, items such as patents, licences, trade marks, logos, brands etc. For some businesses these may be incidental, while in other cases they are key to the performance and potential of that business. Consider companies operating in the pharmaceutical, biotechnology and information technology areas, for instance. Well-known brands can be virtually priceless.

We normally expect a brand to demonstrate its value in terms of earnings generated. It may, however, be under-exploited by its current owners and capable of creating considerable additional earnings in the hands of, say, a large marketing-driven organisation with the financial strength to promote the brand aggressively. Where a strong buyer identifies such an opportunity, he will reflect it in his offer.

Valuation of intangibles can be very difficult but also very significant.

Remember – transactions take place when the business is more valuable to the buyer than to the seller.

Current comparisons

No valuation can be completed without taking account of the current economic scene and outlook, both national and international, where this is applicable. In addition, we must consider the outlook for the market sector in which your business operates. The merger and acquisition field is very much a fashion business, as all those in estate agencies or in the retail sector will readily acknowledge.

We must take into account the evidence offered by recent transactions affecting similar companies. These are, after all, the acid test. However, you need to exercise considerable care to make sure that the transactions compared are relevant and valid. Knowing the full background to such transactions is often vital, both in terms of assessing the relative needs and objectives of both parties, and in understanding the form of consideration passing. All too often details reported in the press of such transactions are incomplete and may indeed be misleading. One or two significant examples will be cited later in this book.

The cluster effect

Having considered such major areas we will try to arrive at a consensus or 'cluster' of values. This is where we must apply judgement rather than pure mathematics. Financial calculations can take us so far but will be no substitute for careful judgement in the final stages.

The valuation of a leasing company in Chapter 9 is a classic illustration of the pitfalls of relying purely on financial or accounting information.

The result will not be a value to the nearest penny but the development of a range of values suggesting the sort of price that we can reasonably expect. Valuing a business is not an exact science.

Chapter 6

Earnings-Based Valuations

Introduction

Having discussed in the previous chapter the broad approach to valuing your business, it is time to look in more detail at some of the specific methods used. Since most businesses are purchased for their earnings potential, it is natural to consider earnings and, in particular, likely future earnings as the first basis of any valuation.

In a few cases, cash flow may be more significant than reported profits or earnings. This topic will be considered in Chapter 9.

In developing an earnings-based valuation we must work through four distinct steps:

- The historical record of earnings
- The estimate of maintainable earnings
- The appropriate earnings multiples to use
- The calculation of value ranges.

The values derived will be compared to those reached by other methods, discussed in later chapters, to achieve a consensus or 'cluster' of valuations. Where these are close, we can have a fairly high degree of confidence in our estimates. Where differences are substantial, they can only be resolved by careful judgement.

Historical earnings

We all recognise that historical earnings are certainly not an infallible guide to future profitability. In most ongoing businesses, however, they are indicative of the profit potential, particularly the results of the last three to four years.

Patterns and trends can often be discerned which, taken in conjunction with other factors, can help to form reasonable projections of future profits and must therefore be considered of significant value.

Where we are dealing with a start-up or recently formed company, however, or where earnings show considerable volatility, obviously this method is less valuable.

Defining real profits

First, we take great care to define ongoing profits or earnings. These are profits that arise from the normal operation of the business and it is necessary to extract and disregard one-off windfalls unless these are, in effect, a regularly recurring pattern for the business.

Equally, we may have to add back extraordinary losses as long as these are genuine one-off losses. It is always tempting to treat windfall or extraordinary profits as regular operating profits, and therefore to be left in the profit calculations, while regarding any unusual loss as essentially a one-off to be added back. I have seen considerable ingenuity used in defending such practices. In fact, we have to look objectively and rationally at any such extraordinary items where these are material or important to the profits record.

In calculating real earnings we add back at this stage all benefits and payments to the owner and his family. These benefits can take many different forms and would include salaries, pension contributions, motor expenses, travel, entertainment, club fees and so on. In the jargon of the trade we call these 'directors' depredations'. We charge instead an arm's-length remuneration package in their place.

This means that we must identify how many salaried managers would be required to run the business in the absence of the owner and his family, and then estimate the total remuneration packages that such managers would need to attract them into the business in purely employment positions.

Any executive recruitment agency can quickly give you an idea of the size of package you would have to pay to attract a suitable manager for your business, and this will normally include, in addition to salary, a car and health and pension benefits.

In calculating directors' depredations, we would examine all expenses incurred by the owners and add these back unless they are 'wholly, necessarily and exclusively' incurred for the promotion of the business. Where there is *any* element of benefit to the owner it should be added back.

This seems rational and reasonable and yet in practice it can become a most emotive issue to the owner. I have met many owners, conditioned perhaps by 83 per cent tax rates, who believed that everything they did had to be absolutely first class and without regard to cost. A Rolls-Royce car would be the absolute minimum to create the required impression when visiting customers or trade associates. Their wife, or perhaps a decorously elegant secretary, must always accompany them on overseas trips to ensure that they travel in the right frame of mind. However difficult, it is in everyone's interest to be realistic with regard to these add-backs and to be prepared to document and defend the adjustments.

There can, of course, be offsetting adjustments. An example would be an adjustment for the use by the business of freehold property belonging personally to the owner. The company may operate out of an office/warehouse complex worth £1 million belonging to the owner or his family who charge no rent for the facilities. In a case like this, a market rent must be 'imputed' and deducted from all years' profit figures to arrive at adjusted earnings unless the property is to be included in the sale.

At this stage, we would normally disregard investment income from earnings calculations and consider the value of the investments separately when valuing the assets.

It may be that the owner has loaned money to the company. Where he is charging a commercial rate of interest on this loan no adjustment is required. If no interest is charged, it may be better to treat the loan effectively as additional equity for valuation purposes and make no adjustment to the profits in this respect. The buyer will, in any case, normally wish to settle all indebtedness due to or from the vendors at completion.

It is by no means unusual for there to be a big difference between reported earnings and real or adjusted earnings. This suggests no impropriety on the part of the owners – after all, this is a private company and managers and shareholders are often one and the same. If they choose to pay Aunt Sally £20,000 per annum for representing the company, who are we to dispute it? Certainly the calculation of profits or earnings from a tax point of view is an entirely separate matter, for discussion and agreement with the tax inspector. As long as he gets his 'pound of flesh' he could not care less.

For a calculation of adjusted profits, see the example given on page 51.

Maintainable earnings

To form a better overview of the company's performance, it is a good idea to summarise on one sheet turnover, cost of sales, gross income or margin, fixed overhead, interest expense and adjusted profit before tax, for the last three or four years. For the current year, assuming, for instance, we are half way through the year, a reasonable projection could be made for the full 12-month period. It would be ideal also if you projected similar figures for one full year ahead. Refer to the example on page 52.

In the latest full year you will note that reported profits of £135,000 have been adjusted to a real £385,000. This is not untypical.

This summary information should now be examined carefully to detect trends, patterns or inconsistencies. Many buyers will look carefully at gross margins in particular, and will query the reasons for any significant variances.

Ideally, the picture over four to five years of both actual and projected results will reveal a steadily improving performance with good stability and will show separately any extraordinary profits or losses. Be prepared to defend your conclusions that these are, indeed, one-off, isolated, adjustments. At this stage we should ignore corporate income taxes.

ARTHUR DAVEY LIMITED
CALCULATION OF ADJUSTED PROFITS

Year to 31 December	£	1991 £
Profits reported on draft accounts before tax		135,000
Add back:		
Arthur Davey Salary	145,000	
Arthur Davey Pension contributions	54,400	
Arthur Davey Bonus	18,000	
Arthur Davey NIC	24,000	
Arthur Davey Club fees	2,300	
Arthur Davey Entertainment and travel	11,800	
Arthur Davey Telephone and sundries	3,300	
Mrs A Davey Salary	23,000	
Mrs A Davey NIC	2,500	
Mrs John Low Salary (sister-in-law)	10,000	
Mrs John Low NIC	1,100	
Motor vehicles (5)	39,300	
Housekeeper's costs	18,800	353,500
		488,500
Deduct:		
Notional rent charge on offices owned by Mr Davey – as per surveyor's valuation	36,000	
Arm's-length management charges: Managing director @ £45,000 pa + commission, health and pension contributions	55,000	
Junior secretary and benefits	12,500	103,500
Adjusted profit for valuation purposes		**385,000**

ARTHUR DAVEY LIMITED
SUMMARY OF TRADING RESULTS AND ADJUSTED PROFITS

(£000)

Year to 31 December	1988	1989	1990	1991	1992
Status of figures	Audited	Audited	Audited	Draft	Forecast
Turnover	4,350	4,600	5,150	5,300	5,900
Variable/direct costs	2,570	2,682	2,987	3,339	3,740
Gross margin	1,780	1,918	2,163	1,961	2,160
(as a percentage)	(40.9)	(41.7)	(42.0)	(37.0)	(36.7)
Overhead costs	1,660	1,908	2,018	1,826	1,980
Pretax profit (after deducting items below)	120	10	145	135	180
Extraordinary profits (losses) (included above)		(125)			
Adjustments for directors' depredations (net)	240	255	285	250	260
Adjusted pretax profit	360	390	430	385	440
Average adjusted profit (maintainable earnings)					£401,000 say £400,000

Notes

1. 1991 proved a difficult trading year. Turnover was increased slightly at cost to margins. Margins are slowly improving in 1992.
2. At June 1992, although actual turnover and profits are only 5 per cent ahead of forecast, prices are firming and management are convinced the forecast can be achieved by December.
3. Extraordinary loss was owing to subsidence at factory not fully covered by insurance.
4. Adjustments for directors' drawings are detailed on the Calculation of Adjusted Profits chart.

Be careful of projecting dramatic upturns in turnover and profits in the years to come. In all too many future earnings projections, profits tend to soar off into the wide blue yonder next year and the year after.

By examining these adjusted profit figures for the last two or three years, plus the current year and one year ahead, it should be possible to make a reasonable estimate of maintainable earnings for the business. Because of the inherent lack of precision, however, it may be preferable to express these earnings as a range, say, 10 per cent below and 10 per cent above the arithmetical average figure calculated.

Ask yourself, do I believe these figures – particularly the forward projections? Many an informed buyer will develop a purchase formula based on these projections. If they are hopelessly optimistic you may be fashioning a noose to hang yourself, because he may make part of the price dependent on your being able to achieve these profits for him.

In the example I have calculated a maintainable earnings value of £400,000 per annum.

Price/Earnings multiples and ratios

We must now develop average price/earnings ratios or earnings multiples for publicly quoted companies in your industry sector, refine them for your company and use them in conjunction with the earnings figures to calculate a value for your business.

There are a number of reasons put forward for adopting this approach:

- the level of risks and the perception of potential and related rewards required should be comparable for similar companies in the same industry sector;
- the multiples enjoyed by public companies will automatically reflect the borrowing costs appropriate to that sector;
- it is probable that trade buyers for your company will emerge from this group and, even if they do not eventually succeed in purchasing the company, they will tend to set the pace for others to follow. They might, in effect, provide a 'fallback' bid.

Like all broad assumptions, however, there are difficulties in following this line of thought.

For one thing, it is difficult to find a truly comparable company or industry sector. Company size varies, the way companies are financed differs and their activity mixes can be dissimilar. It is tempting to force your company into a mould whether it really fits or not, particularly if the multiples enjoyed by the quoted companies look attractive. This can result in a misleading valuation.

It is also tempting to review the quoted companies in the chosen sector and eliminate those that for one reason or another seem not typical, unfavourable to you or lowly rated. I believe it is better to settle for a pure average for the sector provided that there are, say, a dozen or more companies making up the index.

In some cases comparisons of earnings multiples may simply not be appropriate.

Where your company has adjusted earnings of much less than £100,000 per annum, pretax, I consider comparisons of multiples to be of dubious value. The company is probably too insignificant a player in the market and other valuation methods are more appropriate.

If your company's profits compared to turnover are small, using multiples may again provide misleading results. If, for instance, you have a manufacturing company with a turnover of, say, £10 million per annum and an adjusted net profit before tax of £200,000, it is probably operating on a knife edge. A 2 per cent swing in prices is sufficient to double profits or eliminate them completely. However, this would not be true if you were in, say, commodity trading where taking a small percentage on huge volumes is typical of that activity.

Where your company's results are patchy or particularly where the company swings into losses, averaging these figures may be questionable.

The chart on page 55 shows the development of a suitable industry sector earnings multiple of 8.4 times.

DEVELOPING A PRICE/EARNINGS RATIO

Sector: Building materials

Company	Price	Market capitalisation (£ million)	Yield	P/E
Breedon	88	25.0	7.0	9.0
British Fittings	178	29.6	5.5	8.4
Freeman	70	4.56	16.2	3.6
Grafton	126	19.6	6.0	6.1
Hepworth	374	729.2	5.3	13.9
Johnston	205	21.5	8.5	10.2
Kingspan	72	18.8	3.9	6.8
Lilleshall	98	15.8	5.3	11.1
Newman-Tonks	155	160.2	8.0	13.9
Plastiseal	39	3.06	10.3	5.9
A N Other	95	21.3	6.0	7.5
A N Other	79	41.0	7.3	4.4
				100.8
Divide by number of companies				12.0
Average price/earnings ratio after tax				8.4

– In practice each company chosen would be selected for its comparability to our business. Even in the building materials sector there is a wide range of activities so selectivity is still important.

– Companies with no quoted price/earnings on the day chosen should obviously be excluded rather than allowed to distort the average.

– Where a price/earnings ratio is distorted because of underlying asset cover or a significant or abrupt change in earnings, this should be disregarded wherever possible.

– It would be wrong to 'weight' the average to reflect market capitalisation of companies in the index unless perhaps the most probable buyer was one of two or three of the 'giants' in this sector.

Picking an Appropriate Multiple

We have now calculated an *after-tax* price/earnings ratio or earnings multiple for an average quoted company in your industry sector.

Remember, however, that public companies will be under constant market evaluation by investors and City analysts who are generally provided with a far greater level of information and disclosure than that available in respect of a private company. If the stock market investor does not like what he sees he can quickly and easily 'vote with his feet' and sell out. In addition, the typical quoted company tends to be larger and more diversified than its private cousin and probably has better access to new capital by virtue of its institutional following.

In contrast, with a private company there is usually little or no liquidity in the shares. Selling your shares is not normally just a question of a phone call to your broker, but is dependent on finding a willing buyer. A minority shareholding in a private company in the hands of a passive or non-involved shareholder can be a pathetic thing.

Your company may be small in comparison with the average public company. This implies limited resources, less management depth, less 'fat' to survive downturns in the economy and possibly an over-concentration or reliance on one or two large customers, suppliers or products. In addition, you may have limited access to capital and as a small company your staying power is automatically somewhat suspect. The company may also be heavily reliant on one or two key individuals.

In addition, because a private company is out of the public eye and is more difficult to follow or, indeed, locate, it tends to be less appreciated.

For all these reasons the typical private business will not command the multiple that its public cousin will enjoy.

Therefore, we talk about 'discounting' or reducing the sector multiple to reflect these considerations. This is not, incidentally, applicable only to private companies; there are many smaller publicly quoted companies which would also suffer by comparison. Some of these were introduced via the

Unlisted Securities Market originally, and there may be a very small 'float' or percentage of shares actively traded by the public. These companies will also not generally enjoy the advantageous multiples of their bigger brethren unless their prospects are truly exceptional.

On the other hand, there are factors which might suggest that a higher or better multiple should be awarded to your company.

Earnings may be strong and growing steadily; they may typically be growing at twice the industry average. Note that it is *not* enough to grow at the industry average. If a small company is to make progress, it must expand at a faster rate, since incremental increases may prove more and more difficult to achieve as the company becomes larger.

Your company might have some promising products or interesting market niches offering tremendous potential. Increasing turnover by £2 million to £3 million at good margins might well make a significant difference to your profits. Such an increase, of course, would go unnoticed in British Petroleum's figures.

There may be many other potential attractions. Some of these intangibles are more fully discussed in Chapter 8.

You can make a list of comparative advantages and disadvantages of your company *vis-à-vis* the average sector public company and then try to assess a discount or premium factor for each consideration. I believe, however, that carried too far this creates a spurious impression of precision and, after all, at the end it all comes down to judgement.

I recommend adopting a limited number of factors for your consideration and suggest some pointers and comments. These are shown on the chart on page 58 for your convenience. Work through them for your company, but be realistic!

Principal factors affecting probable discount

1. Size

All other things being equal, if the company is of the size that it could readily go for a public flotation, a discount attributable

ARTHUR DAVEY LIMITED

CALCULATING AN APPROPRIATE PRICE/EARNINGS RATIO OR MULTIPLE

Average after-tax price/earnings multiple for your sector (see chart on p. 55)   8.4x

Adjust for following factors:

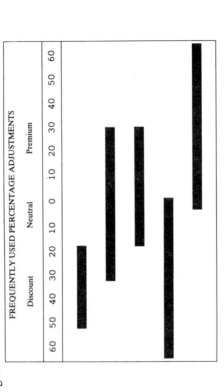

	FREQUENTLY USED PERCENTAGE ADJUSTMENTS			
	Discount	Neutral	Premium	
	60 50 40 30 20 10 0 10 20 30 40 50 60			
SIZE				(30%)
GROWTH				0%
MANAGEMENT				10%
DIVERSIFICATION				(30%)
INTANGIBLES				20%
				(30%)
				5.9x

Comments

1. Size – reasonable turnover, margins and profits but not big enough to float publicly.
2. Modest growth in difficult period.
3. Good management team capable of better things under stronger support and guidance.
4. Diversification – not significantly at risk.
5. Some attractive new products under development.

to a private company in this case may be of the order of 10–15 per cent. This implies demonstrated earnings levels pretax of, say, £1.5 million to £2 million per annum. The discount used probably reflects the costs of bringing the company to the market. On the other hand, a company earning £200,000–£300,000 per annum pretax could not normally go for a public quotation, and on that basis alone the multiple applicable may be discounted by 30–40 per cent.

2. Earnings and growth

Declining earnings or gross margins and, especially, actual losses incurred, unless these are mirrored throughout the industry, will certainly suggest a significant discount on the average public company's multiple and this would again typically be 30–40 per cent. Your company will have to enjoy very good margins and strong earnings growth and potential to rate a multiple equal to the industry sector.

3. Management

The weighting for this factor will, in practice, largely be determined by the buyer. A knowledgeable trade buyer with spare management capacity may have confidence in his ability to assume control of the new business smoothly and efficiently. The quality of your management is, therefore, of less importance to him. On the other hand, the buyer might look to your managers to strengthen his own organisation.

A non-trade buyer will be attracted by other features, for example, the opportunity to enter a new market sector or to secure steady earnings, and may assign considerable importance to the quality of the management team in place.

4. Diversification and risk

This will usually be seen by the buyer as a negative factor or risk and rarely as a positive one for negotiation purposes, at least. Excessive reliance on one supplier, customer, product or market could suggest higher risk and a less attractive situation, hence the discount.

Unusual attractions

Since beauty or, in this case, value is in the eye of the beholder (buyer), you may only be able to guess at the features of your business which would make it attractive to a buyer. These attractions are intangibles and are discussed in Chapter 8. They can, however, make a significant difference to the sales price achieved.

Essentially, if your business has a refined product, service, reputation or market niche with 'sex appeal' or potential for profitable exploitation in the hands of the buyer, he may be prepared to pay a substantial premium to gain control.

We recently sold a business which was only one of three suppliers in the world making small speciality fittings for use in environmental clean-up equipment. The owners did not have the organisation, financial muscle or, indeed, the energy, to take the product line to the next logical stage of its development. The buyer was a public company with all these skills, plus an entry to the prime market for the new products being developed, and paid a healthy premium for control.

A weighting is now assigned to these factors and applied to the *industry sector earnings multiple* to calculate a multiple for use with your company.

Work through the example given on page 58. This produces a multiple of 5.9 times.

Calculation of earnings-based values

We have adjusted and analysed your company's earnings for the last three or four years and have projected ahead for 18 months to develop annual maintainable earnings.

We have established an industry sector earnings multiple appropriate for your area of activity and have considered your trading advantages and disadvantages compared to the average company in the sector. The industry/price earnings multiple has been discounted or reduced to reflect these differences, and we are now ready to calculate a valuation based on earnings.

There is one other point to be borne in mind before we can make our calculation.

We must remember that publicly quoted earnings multiples are on an *after-tax* basis, whereas the maintainable earnings calculated for your company are pretax. To put the maintainable earnings on to an after-tax basis, we must adjust for corporate taxes at the standard (buyer's) rate. Assuming a 33 per cent corporate rate, this means multiplying the maintainable profits (£400,000) by 67 per cent. This produces £268,000. Note that although your company may pay tax at the small company rate of 25 per cent, the likelihood is that the buyer will pay at the full corporate rate of 33 per cent.

We are now in a position to complete the calculation.

1. We have taken the company's reported earnings and have adjusted to a 'stand alone' basis. The adjusted profits for the years 1988–92 range from £360,000 to £440,000. A maintainable earnings figure pretax of *£400,000* has been taken.
2. Converting this to an after-tax profit, assuming a tax rate of 33 per cent, we realise, say, *£268,000*.
3. Selecting the most appropriate industry sector from the financial press, we have calculated an average price/earnings ratio of *8.4* times.
4. Considering the main areas of the company's weaknesses and strengths, we have developed a discount factor of *30 per cent*. This is a judgement factor.
5. Applying this discount factor to the average price/earnings ratio in point 3 above, we achieve a price/earnings factor for your company of *5.9* times.
6. Therefore, to calculate the value of your company on an earnings basis, multiply 5.9 × £268,000, which gives you **£1,581,000**.
7. This suggests a value range of £1,500,000 to £1,600,000.

Summary

We have now valued the company on the basis of earnings, through the eyes of a trade buyer who is a predictable suitor for your hand when it is time to sell. In practice, a trade buyer will normally set the pace and underpin any bidding. It would be unwise to calculate values based on premium or 'jigsaw' buyers, since there is no guarantee that you can find one when you decide to sell.

Remember that a buyer will prefer smooth earnings growth and will distrust violent swings in profits. You should keep extraordinary adjustments to a minimum and be prepared to defend these very specifically when challenged. Where a buyer detects any weakness or 'sponginess' in the treatment of extraordinary profits, losses or other adjustments, it will tend to undermine his confidence in all your explanations.

We have assumed that the buying company will probably suffer tax at the standard rate, ie 33 per cent, and we have used *this rate* as the basis for our calculations. We have disregarded the actual corporate taxes paid by your company and concentrated on pretax earnings.

Chapter 7

Asset-Based Valuations

Introduction

We have previously considered valuations based on profits or earnings. We will now look at valuations based on the net assets of the business. For the purposes of this chapter, we consider only tangible assets: assets you can touch, measure or record. The next chapter will be devoted to a discussion of intangibles, including brands, patents, licences and so on.

A nice little earner

Consider the following similarly sized businesses:

1. Arthur Davey has a used car business and his stock consists of £1 million worth of Jaguars, Rovers and Mercedes, all purchased at trade auctions across the country. He pays cash for purchases and, let us assume, receives cash for all sales. Therefore, the net asset value of the business is represented by cars with a trade value of £1 million. The business has a solid record of producing £50,000 a year of real profits for Arthur.

   On, say, a 5 times multiple, as discussed in Chapter 6, Arthur's business is worth £250,000. However, Arthur is unlikely to sell for that price, even if he does want to dispose of the business. He calculates that he can quickly and easily achieve £1 million selling all his stock in the trade.

2. Arthur's brother Geoff Davey runs a small engineering company producing run-of-the-mill products. His net assets, which comprise typically plant, machinery and

equipment, loose tools, stock, spare parts and work in progress, together with the normal spread of debtors and creditors, total £1 million. The company is also making for Geoff Davey a steady profit of £50,000 a year on turnover, let us say, of £3–£4 million.

On an earnings multiple basis, we would again value the business, using a 5 times multiple, at £250,000. While Geoff Davey may not accept £250,000 for his business, he might consider himself lucky indeed to achieve a sale at £1 million or at full net asset value.

A potential buyer of his business must continue to run that business to make use of the assets employed. If Geoff Davey were to cease trading, he would experience great difficulty recovering £1 million from a sale of the assets, even though the replacement value might well be £1.5 million.

The moral here is that there are assets and assets.

How easy is it to convert assets to cash?

Generally, if the net assets of a business are readily convertible into cash, the vendor always has the option of doing just that and realising his investment quickly at relatively low cost. Examples of such a business would include distributors, traders, wine merchants and so on.

Provided there are no potential liabilities arising owing to speculation or open contracts, the value of the business is the net asset value of the stock less the costs of realisation and, perhaps, a discount for delays in receiving the cash. The more difficult it is to realise and convert the assets into cash, or the more protracted the process, the higher the risk. All these factors will be reflected in the value of that business.

There is, therefore, a range of asset valuations varying from a business in which the assets are relatively liquid or easily 'encashable' to a business composed in a large part of difficult-to-sell plant and machinery, work in progress, ageing debtors, excess stocks and so on.

Assets as an integral part of the business

How are we then to value business assets which are worth book value only as part of a dynamic business?

In this case, the first question to determine is whether the company is commercially viable. The real test here is cash flow rather than reported profits since, as we all know, businesses collapse from a lack of cash not from a lack of profits.

Where the business is supported by a parent company or by a wealthy shareholder lending his name to bank guarantees etc, and where the business is dependent on such support, we must look at the question of its viability carefully.

This support might take various forms. It might be inter-company lending at a zero rate of interest, whereas under new owners the funds represented by that inter-company debt would have to be replaced by bank financing at 15 per cent per annum.

Alternatively, the parent company, or shareholders, may provide premises or other services below cost or supply raw materials at advantageous prices. As an independent, stand-alone business, it would not receive these benefits and might no longer be commercially viable.

The value of any such support will not only be taken into account when calculating adjusted profits in Chapter 6 but will also influence the values we can put on assets employed in the business.

In most cases, therefore, there is an essential linkage between assets and profits or cash flow generated. Where the business is operating successfully on a self-sustaining basis, asset valuations can be carried out with confidence on an existing use basis. Where it cannot operate independently, all such calculations are hypothetical.

Equally, the transformation of a loss-making or break-even business into a profitable one by an experienced company doctor will transform the value of the assets employed.

The impact of borrowings

Consider two companies both with net assets of £1 million.

Let us assume that Company A has no bank borrowings, whereas Company B has bank overdrafts and loans totalling, say, £1 million. (Note that Company B still has £1 million of net assets *after* deducting liabilities to the bank).

Logically, all other things being equal, we would ascribe a similar asset value to both businesses, but remember that assets are generally regarded as 'soft' and liabilities, especially secured liabilities, are 'hard'.

In this case, all other things being equal, a buyer will instinctively rate Company A more valuable to him since its assets are free and 'unencumbered'. He will worry that the bank will have security over or a 'hook into' all assets of value in Company B, thus diminishing its attractiveness to a new owner.

Adjusting the balance sheet

The chart on page 67 is a work-sheet detailing adjustments made to audited accounts to calculate the real value of net tangible assets for the purposes of our valuation.

The starting point might well be draft unaudited accounts since an owner thinking of selling may defer finalising decisions on dividends, pension contributions and so on until a sale is agreed.

The chart contains a real hotchpotch of adjustments provided for illustrative purposes. You may find these helpful in stimulating thoughts about your own business, although in real life we might be horrified to have to make so many adjustments.

While many of the adjustments will be self-explanatory, additional comments will be useful.

1. The net asset value taken is that figure equal to the shareholders' recorded investment in the company – as represented by share capital, share premiums, revenue and capital reserves.

GEOFFREY DAVEY LIMITED
ADJUSTMENT OF NET ASSET VALUES
as at 31/5/92

			£
Net asset values as at 31/12/91, audited accounts			1,526,321

Add:	Adjustment for freehold property.
	    Valuation on an open market
	    basis dated 15/10/91
		£650,000	

	Less: Book value	475,000	175,000
	Net profits to date for period 1/1/92 to 31/5/92	186,000	
	Less: Provision for corporation taxes @ 33%	61,000	125,000

	Amount due to associated
	    company (liability not assumed
	    by purchaser)
			74,000

	Increase in value of stock and
	    work in progress following
	    physical inventory at 31/5/92
	    (agreed between auditors)
			30,000

			1,930,321
Deduct:	Under-provision of depreciation on plant and machinery		(80,000)
	Other investments – to be retained by vendor (book value)		(150,000)
	Goodwill recorded in accounts (book value)		(35,000)
	Additional provision required for specific doubtful debts – agreed between parties		(27,000)
	Personal loan due from shareholder (not assumed by purchaser)		(46,000)
	Market value of motor vehicles to be retained by vendors		(32,000)

	Pension contributions to be made by the
	    company on behalf of owners prior to
	    completion
			(250,000)

	Cash dividend declared in April 1992		(100,000)
	Estimated liability not provided for in respect of current legal case outstanding		(40,000)
	Adjusted net asset value		£1,170,321

All debts due to and from the owners, or to other companies controlled by them should be added back as adjustments, as has been done in this illustration. No buyer is going to pay for debts due to the company by the previous owners and risk having difficulty collecting later.

2. Where the valuation is being done at a date other than the company's financial year-end and no interim audit carried out, an adjustment would be made for subsequent profits and taxes. This is, of course, common when actually selling the company but unusual when carrying out a valuation.

3. Where you would retain certain assets – like motor cars or investments – or propose paying out dividends or pension contributions, these must be deducted.

4. Amounts recorded as goodwill must also be deducted – the buyer's calculations will eventually reveal the value of goodwill, and indeed other intangibles, if any, in the business. Historic goodwill balances have no value to the valuer at this stage.

5. Any unrecorded or 'off-balance sheet' liabilities must be deducted at a fair estimate of the probable cost. If a current legal case could cost £40,000 to settle you might as well recognise this at the outset.

Now let us look at the possible classes of asset that we must consider in any valuation:

1. Freehold property (including land and buildings, lease premiums and leasehold improvements)

Until recently this was the banker's favourite asset providing apparently excellent security for any loans, and on a par, almost, with gold dust. Some owners will even inject freehold property into the company to provide a suitable asset base and give it a more acceptable financial profile.

The property may have been purchased in 1935 and is still carried in the books at its historical value. It may even have been depreciated since then.

It is more likely to have been revalued, however, and in this case a buyer will certainly want to know when it was revalued, by whom and on what basis. Does the valuer have a good reputation and does he know the local market? What does the valuation actually say? Many valuations turn out to be optimistic expressions of opinion.

The value of lease premiums will reflect the present value of short-term benefits where agreed rental is lower than market value. This value will decline as the lease period expires and can fluctuate and even disappear where demand for space in that area evaporates.

Unless premises have been significantly improved by the tenant and there is a long lease remaining, it may be difficult to recover any consideration for leasehold improvements effected. They are generally not removable.

Valuations may cite 'replacement cost' (properly only an insurance term) which can be a real red herring. Your wife's engagement ring may have a replacement cost today at £2000 but your local jeweller may be unwilling to offer more than £250 for it. That is the attraction for the less scrupulous members of our society in selling their business to the insurance company.

The valuation may cite existing-use basis, ie the value to that business which, again, is fine if your business is viable and profitable. A forced-sale valuation, with vacant possession, will only be applicable in desperate circumstances where the company's continued survival is under question.

Alternatively, if you are thinking seriously of selling the business, you may decide not to include the property in the sale but to retain it and derive a retirement income from the rent it provides. There are both opportunities and dangers in this course of action and these will be discussed later in Chapter 14.

In my experience, good businessmen will generally prefer to buy businesses and business assets rather than invest in freehold property. They will argue that they are in business to make money from the assembly and sale of, say, medical equipment, not in the field of property speculation. This, incidentally, is a prevalent attitude among European buyers, but is still not nearly so common in the UK.

If a property is owned by you personally, make sure that a market rent is being charged in computing the profits of your business.

2. Plant and machinery

This comes, of course, in all shapes and sizes. Some plant and machinery is easily removable and saleable. To remove other equipment you would have to demolish the building first.

It may be that the equipment is specialised and difficult to find. Perhaps the only manufacturer of this equipment has a small production line in Switzerland and is quoting 18 months delivery. In these cases, plant and equipment can have substantial value, particularly where they are closely associated with profitable end products in considerable demand.

On the other hand, some of your plant and equipment may weigh 20 or 30 tons and date back to the Victorian age. It may be dedicated to present processes, producing products for a declining market, and may be difficult to move, service or repair. Unfortunately, it may have more value as scrap.

You will have been depreciating this equipment over the years and, provided that sensible depreciation rates have been used, it should be in the books at a modest figure.

However, some companies are fond of revaluing such assets from time to time to give a boost to the balance sheet. The problem here is that any significant increase in value will increase depreciation charged against profits. A slow rate of write off, achieved through low depreciation rates, will improve the bottom line but will often be challenged by potential purchasers. While both straight line and declining balance methods of depreciation have their applicability and adherents, any move to a declining balance rate of, say, 10 per cent per annum will be questioned during negotiations. It can take for ever to write the asset off.

Competition is forcing companies to update equipment all the time and often plant more than five years old may be of questionable value. This is particularly true where plant is dependent, for instance, on computerised controls which may be upgraded every two to three years.

We have one client in a hyper-competitive textile sector

that regularly disposes of equipment after three years, shipping it, in fact, to US textile manufacturers and replacing it with the latest technology.

Modern equipment tends to provide much more flexibility for making rapid and inexpensive changes of design or product and minimising down-time, labour involvement and cost. The market is becoming too competitive for most companies to survive producing goods on 10- to 20-year-old equipment.

3. Motor vehicles

Many private companies over-invest in motor cars. It is not unusual to come across a company with 35 or 40 employees and 15 or 20 cars. We suspect that when the government blandly talks about imports of plant and equipment adding to our trading account difficulties, they are lumping in investment in motor cars which is often a luxury item.

Fortunately, it is relatively easy to place a value on your fleet of motor vehicles. There is an efficient resale market in the UK thanks to auction houses and car buying magazines. There are also a number of good guides to current trade prices.

Again, one should ask which of the vehicles are absolutely essential to the business and which, in effect, are surplus.

4. Stocks, inventory and work in progress

A lot of print has been devoted to the valuation of stocks, inventories, work in progress and similar assets. Suffice it to say that you will be expected to operate sensible ageing and write-down policies providing fully for old or slow-moving stocks. This is particularly true where your inventory is composed of fashion or semi-fashion items. Nothing is less attractive or less saleable than yesterday's newspaper.

Surprisingly, in the present difficult market, even staple products like industrial fasteners can be worth considerably less than cost owing to over-supply or lack of demand.

Where the business is fully viable and the inventory levels are appropriate to that industry sector, it should not be too difficult to form reasonable valuations. However, where inventory is excessive or where work in progress is dedicated to particular customers who are not legally required to take it, we must use considerable caution.

The sheer amount of stock alone may determine the value. If your company is in shoe distribution and has a million pairs of summer shoes in September, you have to be a little nervous. In such a case recently, we came across a bank valuing a consumer goods inventory at 15 per cent of cost, or something like 10 per cent of retail value. I suppose you can always ship them to Australia and hope they have a long summer.

Work in progress is, of course, particularly difficult to value since, by definition, further processing is required before the product becomes saleable. Again, the viability of a company in such a case and its ability to continue must be unquestioned.

5. Trade debtors

The same comments would apply here as to stock and work in progress. Obviously, any well-run company has a process of credit control, ageing, writing down or providing against doubtful debtors, and a buyer will predictably look carefully at the balances on your trade ledger.

He will certainly focus on large debts, particularly monies owed by companies that may be suspect. He will examine payment histories of such customers. Where your customer has an ongoing requirement for essential services which cannot easily be met elsewhere, this will tend to improve the collectability of the debts.

6. Off-balance sheet assets

When evaluating the business consider also the off-balance sheet items – items which do not appear on the balance sheet. We have referred above to liabilities but what about assets?

One example will illustrate the point. A company purchasing and installing vending machines may sell these outright to its customers taking the profit on sale directly into its accounts.

However, it is not uncommon to install and service equipment on the basis of, say, a five-year non-cancellable contract.

In this case, a real asset of the business, which may or may not be on the books, is the value of a stream of contract payments anticipated in future. Collection of these may well involve servicing costs and the net present value of the contracts is certainly less than the aggregate value owing to timing, credit risks and so on. It can, however, still represent a significant asset to the buyer and one to be reflected in the valuation.

Relationship of assets to earnings

Remember in all these cases, however, that assets tend to be 'soft', ie prone to difficulties in realisation or collection whereas liabilities tend to be 'hard', especially those which have been charged to a lender.

In reviewing the assets used and their values, ask yourself how critical they are to the success of the business. Would you have to replace them? Would you do so in the same quantities and in the same quality? If not, substitute the amount you could realise by selling them, taking into account realistic costs of sale, for the values in the accounts.

The much maligned asset stripper may well be performing a public service by buying a company and stripping out all the assets which are not required to run that business. He may be redeploying the funds realised from the sale of those assets to expand in other directions.

You will now be adding up the values of all the essential assets used in the business and substituting sale prices for the rest.

For the buyer to justify paying your price for those assets he will want to see a return of at least 20–25 per cent pretax on his investment, assuming prime bank rates running at, say, 10–12 per cent per annum. If the maintainable annual earnings that we calculated in the previous chapter already exceed 20 per cent of the net asset values, these values will underpin any earnings-based valuation of the company and we may be looking at something for goodwill.

What if maintainable earnings do not reach 20 per cent of the value we have calculated? Here we may have a problem.

If the tangible assets are all gold dust, or second-hand cars, you are still going to seek 95 per cent net asset value as the price of the business, allowing 5 per cent for collecting and selling off the gold dust and converting it into cash. If, however, you have a much more typical business with a typical mixed bag of assets, the value of the assets would be discounted downwards towards a value required to sustain a 20–25 per cent pretax return.

If the business is earning in excess of 20 per cent per annum on the net asset value, there is an intrinsic value to the business as a business and a goodwill factor is emerging.

If the business is earning less than 20 per cent on the assets employed, to the extent that it falls short, a 'bad-will' factor is emerging. This means that the saleable value of the business, or the purchase price a buyer will pay, is going to tend to drop towards the value that will generate a 20 or 25 per cent level of return.

Before trying to work out exactly where that level is going to come in this case, let us move on to consider the value of intangible assets and we can then pull together all three areas of consideration and start to draw some conclusions.

Chapter 8

Intangible Assets

A wild card

You do all the return on investment or yield calculations, discounted cash flows, earnings multiples, net asset value adjustments etc, but your valuation can be blown right out of the window by intangibles. These range from patents, licences, trade marks and other 'intellectual property', to brands, niche products, specific locations – in fact, a whole range of potential advantages and benefits available to the purchaser.

These should be treated separately from the usual bricks and mortar, equipment, inventory etc that we considered in the last chapter because they are intangible and difficult, if not impossible, to quantify and record. That is not to say, however, that these assets cannot be of considerable value.

Let us look at some examples:

1. Sauce

Imagine that you own the legal rights and know-how pertaining to HP Sauce. Familiar as we all are with the hearty, full English breakfast, we can all picture the HP Sauce bottle on the table at breakfast, at a time perhaps of lowest resistance or maximum suggestibility. HP Sauce is actually owned by BSN of France, a large food group. (We must be thankful, I suppose, that they have not substituted the Eiffel Tower for the Houses of Parliament on the label!)

There are, perhaps, 100 manufacturers in the UK who can formulate, prepare, bottle and deliver this sauce anywhere you like for, let us say, 50p a bottle.

Equally there is a marketing organisation well aware of the strength of the brand name which will guarantee to buy 5 million bottles a year from you at £1 a bottle with that magic name.

Assuming you are merely an intermediary, you do not need a computer to calculate your annual transfer fee at £2.5 million per annum, or 5 million bottles at 50p profit per bottle, and that is just the UK – other countries too have been known to use HP Sauce.

This is obviously a simplistic example but what is the possession of such a brand name worth – £10 million, £20 million, £30 million? Certainly it is a valuable asset although it may not appear as such on a balance sheet. In all probability, the value of the brand is being realised already in terms of profit streams to the lucky owner and, therefore, we might expect the value of the brand to be reflected in a sensible earnings-based valuation of that business.

2. Instruments

Let us consider another example, one drawn from our own records.

Years ago we identified a small medical instrument manufacturer run by two technical 'boffins'. The company had a turnover of £3 million per annum, net asset value of £300,000, and was essentially breaking even after the profits were recalculated, as described in previous chapters.

The owners believed they needed an additional £150,000 to promote further research and development, although a quick check revealed that they were five years ahead of the market even then. The equipment was being sold worldwide to conservative customers – doctors and surgeons who relied on it for the performance of their duties. The average doctor will not seek to change an instrument that is serving him well, even though there may be more modern electronic 'gizmos' on the market.

It turned out that there were over 20,000 of these instruments in active use around the world worth, perhaps, $5000 each. There was also a regular requirement for servicing or realignment and the company was one of very few with the know-how to carry out this essential maintenance.

The result was a steady stream of equipment returned for servicing from Japan, the USA, Australia and so on. The average service charge was £15–£20. As one service man explained to me, 'we can hardly charge more than that when it is simply a case of using a screwdriver and a couple of measuring instruments'. The fact was that with that level of service cost there was no incentive for users to send them anywhere but back to the UK.

It also transpired that there had not been a price increase on the international market for four to five years, even though currencies had fluctuated significantly in that period. The US distributors, for instance, were insisting that the market would not stand increased prices because of competition and felt it was quite appropriate – in fact, barely worth their while – to settle for a 40 or 50 per cent gross margin.

At the time, we represented an imaginative marketing executive who wished to buy his own business. You can well imagine that such an opportunity proved a gold mine. The company needed modern, effective marketing methods and promotion far more than any further immediate expenditure on research and development.

Looking at the company we did not find value in tangible assets and we certainly did not find it in earnings records. We found value in intangibles – potential and opportunity. Although it was not obvious from a casual perusal of the accounts, the value of the intangibles included:

1. The company name – the product was synonymous with the treatment of certain medical conditions and had been around for 30 years.
2. The reputation and willingness of the manufacturer to stand behind the product and service instruments as required.
3. The size and breadth of the installed base of equipment.
4. The ongoing requirement for after-sales service, with all the inherent marketing possibilities that offered.
5. The entrenched position enjoyed by the product in a conservative, slow changing market.

This company had all the attributes of a 'sleeper' with, in effect, beautiful niche products. In this case, however, the intangibles swamped all conventional measurements based on earnings or assets.

Although the owners of the company were not capitalising

on the advantages offered by these intangibles, this does not mean that those intangibles were worthless. In the hands of a buyer capable of developing or exploiting them fully those intangibles had considerable value.

It is a moot point, of course, how much of the value resides in the ability of the buyer. In real life an astute seller is frequently able to reflect some of that advantage in the price he can obtain for his business, provided the opportunity is properly marketed.

Goodwill

A third example will give a graphic illustration of that ephemeral asset called goodwill.

A few years ago we looked at a small practice offering specialist professional services in the UK – one of three or four companies catering to that sector. The only apparent assets this company had were two or three typewriters, a couple of desks, a filing cabinet and a telephone system. The owners were non-active, knew little about the business and turned up once a month for management meetings.

One day the professionals who ran the business walked out to set up in competition and the owners were forced to consider their next step.

With little or no knowledge of the professional practice requirements and with their attentions fully taken up with other pursuits, they were tempted to close the business down completely.

While deliberating future action, however, they noticed incoming mail being piled up by the secretaries, much of which was enquiring about the company's services and asking for quotations and so on. These enquiries stemmed from years of advertising in trade journals, listings in Yellow Pages, and the company's brochures – thousands of which were floating around the world. There were even photocopies of photocopies – the ultimate accolade!

On the spur of the moment, the owners decided to hire new experienced staff and asked the secretaries to help bring them up to speed. Within four months, turnover had actually increased by 50 per cent!

That is goodwill. It represents an element of business momentum built up over years of trading contacts and representation such that the activity assumes a life of its own (almost) irrespective of the people carrying out the work.

Something special

You can achieve a reasonably predictable price for your business based on conventional earnings and asset values and, indeed, retire comfortably. However, if your business has something special you can perhaps retire with a fortune, especially if you can pick the right moment to achieve a sale when it might be the flavour of the month.

Will the estate agents who sold out in 1987 or 1988 please go to the head of the class!

It is not always easy to recognise or value these special attributes and in most cases they are not susceptible to precise measurement – so much depends on the buyer and his perceptions, needs or skills. It is well worth working hard, however, to try to identify these attributes when you are valuing your business.

Don't forget that it is not the intrinsic value to you of those intangibles but what they are worth to the *buyer* – value, like beauty, is in the eye of the beholder. The maximum value for your company will be its worth in the hands of a particular buyer. Transactions take place where your business is of more value to the buyer than it is to you – for whatever reason.

Two and two make five

The professionals use that overworked word 'synergy' to describe the whole being greater than the sum of the parts.

Even where the synergy is real, the buyer often has to work hard to realise the full benefits of such an acquisition. Quite properly he will regard those benefits as accruing to him as a result of his efforts and his particular contributions. It is up to you to try to get a slice of that pie by pointing out that without owning your business he'll never make it.

Examples of synergy

We can cite many examples of synergistic opportunities. Let us quote a few so that we are all clear about the possibilities:

1. You own a large lighting equipment retailer in Cardiff and the buyer has a chain of 20 lighting equipment stores across the country, with the exception of South Wales. The purchase of your business gives him a more complete national coverage and he can probably achieve savings on inventory control and purchases, increased turnover and, perhaps, effect economies in the administration and running of your store.

2. You are a manufacturer producing medium-priced photographic enlargers for the amateur. Your suitor also has a range of enlargers and developing equipment but his equipment tends to be more upmarket. By adding your range of equipment to his own there are economies of scale in marketing, distribution, administration, manufacturing etc, resulting in a net profit larger than the original profits of both companies before amalgamation.

3. You produce medications used in conjunction with bandages for the treatment of minor skin ailments. The buyer is a large manufacturer of bandages. There is an obvious match here in that his sales force can be selling and distributing the medication when they sell the bandages that go along with it. This increases the sales force's penetration in the market and improves their effectiveness, resulting in a better bottom line or profit.

4. Recently, we were hired by a European client with a desperate need for additional manufacturing capacity in a particular environmental equipment sector. Research turned up a relatively lacklustre company, but one in exactly the same sector with considerable spare capacity. In this case the intangible asset proved to be the additional capacity which was available at short notice, which effectively increased the value of the company from perhaps £2 million to £3.6 million.

Conclusion

It is surprising that many owners find it difficult to look at their business from the buyer's viewpoint. The range of synergistic opportunities or intangible assets is so vast that this is not an easy thing to conceptualise. But every company owner should do his utmost to identify such advantages or attractions since these will frequently help to clinch a sale or dramatically improve the price achieved. Certainly, when working with a vendor, considerable efforts should be made to identify the widest range of possible benefits to the buyer and highlight these in any preliminary information provided on the company.

In fact, the information 'taster' circulated is normally less an objective recital of earnings and assets and more a document hinting at the potential attractions to the buyer. It is somewhat analogous to the 'dance of the seven veils' in which the dancer is coyly hinting at goodies to come – allowing the buyer full scope to build the picture in his mind that he wants to see.

It is difficult to put a value on such attractions but, unless you make an attempt to do so, your valuation may be fatally flawed.

Chapter 9

Other Valuation Methods

Introduction

Certain businesses do not lend themselves readily to the valuation methods discussed in previous chapters. There are, for instance, professions and trades that have developed specific valuation methods over the years or adopted common yardsticks when valuing or selling businesses.

In addition, there are *lifestyle* businesses where the quality of the lifestyle provided is probably valued more highly by the owner than the actual remuneration derived from that activity.

There are other activities, such as finance or pharmaceuticals, where completely different valuation methods are used, such as *discounted cash flow* which, while appropriate to those businesses, might be inappropriate for other activities.

The purpose of this chapter is to review some of these methods in more detail and to round out the range of valuation techniques to be considered.

Discounted cash flows

With many businesses the levels of sales and profits are highly uncertain and speculative. There are certain commercial sectors, however, where the future turnover, profits and cash flows can be predicted with a high degree of confidence.

Consider, for instance, a leasing company where much of the revenue is derived from non-cancellable lease contracts extending from one to ten years in the future. The actual receipts can be predicted with a great degree of accuracy and the associated funding 'locked in' if desired. Basic administration charges may be a relatively modest part of total expenses.

It follows, therefore, that the net cash flow, or net income, for the next five to ten years can be forecast confidently. In such a case, using appropriate interest rate assumptions, the present value of future profits can be derived and a value for the leasing business or portfolio calculated.

This method is called the discounted cash flow method and can be applicable to other similar businesses, such as finance and mortgage companies, fund management operations etc. Wherever future cash flows can be determined with some accuracy, the discounted cash flow method is appropriate.

It is also widely used in industry for calculating the benefits available from the installation of new equipment or the acquisition of assets, where the additional revenue derived can be predicted with confidence into the future. For example, your business might supply small but vital components to another manufacturer under a long-term contract or, perhaps, a 'take or pay' arrangement. In this case, it might well be appropriate to make a valuation on a discounted cash flow basis.

However, where market demand or prices are unpredictable or where costs, currency fluctuations, obsolescence risks etc make the forecasting of future profits uncertain, this is not a method to be used lightly.

Professionals sometimes value high-risk, highly volatile businesses on a discounted cash flow basis and argue that this is an appropriate method of valuation. But even where your business appears to be perfectly suitable for such a valuation, results are not entirely predictable. One cautionary tale, drawn from my own experience, will illustrate the pitfalls.

Years ago I was involved with a leasing company that was being sold to a bank. The bank's advisers used computers to generate discounted cash flows to establish a present value of the contracts and, indeed, there was a large portfolio of lease agreements involved. These were all with 'blue chip' companies offering what a banker would call a strong covenant, and therefore the risk of non-payment seemed quite low.

I looked on with admiration at reams and reams of computer print-outs covering lease receipts, funding costs etc. With a portfolio of £300 million it was a sizeable exercise. Eventually a transaction was agreed and completed based on the values derived.

Unfortunately, the buyer did not reach an amicable agreement with the chief executive of the company sold and they came to a parting of the ways. Within six months a disgruntled executive had refinanced all the largest and most profitable transactions with other lenders, reducing the real value of the portfolio retained by two-thirds.

When examining the lease contracts no one had thought to verify cancellation or prepayment conditions. In many cases, lessees had options or 'get-out' clauses enabling them to seek lower cost finance without any penalty. The result in this case was one very expensive acquisition.

Property situations

Where the business involved is either a property company or has a large property element, future expectations with regard to property prices will generally outweigh any valuation considerations of the business itself, unless it is a very profitable business indeed. Such companies, of course, will include hotels and restaurants, leisure complexes and schools and, in most cases, the valuations will reflect the underlying property values.

Occasionally, one finds a nice little business run from a property site worth a fortune. In general, it would be better to consider moving the business into leased premises and calculating business values on a stand-alone basis, with rent worked into the calculations if necessary.

There is ambivalence regarding freehold property. Some owners like to include such property in the assets since, traditionally, the banks have been comforted by the perceived security offered by bricks and mortar. Some buyers, however, will spurn the opportunity of acquiring freehold property and comment that they are not in the property business.

Lifestyle businesses

We can all imagine attractive lifestyle businesses. These could range from an upmarket restaurant in a favourite area of town to a travel agency providing cut-price travel for semi-retired owners. We can imagine paying good prices for attractive country estates which provide, or used to provide, in addition to a source of farming income and EC grants, an enviable landed estate lifestyle complete with Range Rovers and green wellies.

Other wealthy individuals may seek out art galleries, speciality book shops or retail shops dealing, for instance, with fashion lines or collectables. In many cases, the purchaser will be motivated not primarily by the amount of income generated but by the desire for that type of lifestyle, allied with some income.

Having sold your engineering business in Birmingham, you may wish to spend your retirement in Devon surrounded by books. You may pay a huge price for a bookshop in Salcombe as a way of achieving both these objectives. Price, within reason, becomes secondary.

At a national or even international level, we are all aware of the acrimonious battles that have taken place for control of Harrods, the celebrated London store, between Lonrho plc and the Al Fayeds. Sothebys and Christies have also been in the news, again largely for prestige or lifestyle considerations.

If you watch television, you may have followed the yachting series *Howard's Way* which became a popular soap opera in the mid-1980s. This was a classic lifestyle business 'soap' and one can readily see why the open-air potential, the excitement of sailing, the attractive locations and companions could lead a wealthy investor into this sector. I know of one millionaire who owns seven yachts which are tucked into suitable lifestyle businesses around the globe.

In all these cases it is impossible to value the underlying business on an objective earnings or asset basis because probable buyers can afford to be capricious and impulsive. They are not basically buying an earning-stream.

These buyers form a small but significant part of our society and they are not in any way constrained by cost and will bid up such a business out of all proportion to its real worth. Their ability and willingness to pay top price for an unusual quality business or property will strike most of us as crazy. In practice, it often pays off handsomely over the longer term, since there is usually an even bigger fish on the horizon looking for something similar. It is a little like musical chairs – fine as long as the music continues.

Just as in the domestic housing market a house in a superb location will always sell, equally an attractive business will not only retain its value but will tend to appreciate more than the run of the mill article.

Competitor elimination

Having made all the reasonable adjustments for asset values and income benefits referred to in previous chapters, suppose you find that your business has no net earnings and no real asset base. How do you value such a company? Is it, in fact, worth anything?

The value of such a business may well be minimal, supplying simply a living to the owner who might be, and often is, sacrificing earnings for the simple privilege of being his own boss and, he hopes, controlling his own destiny. His business may be one of a thousand similar businesses in the UK with no differentiating factors, products or advantages.

What, however, if it is one of only three or four manu-facturers of particular speciality equipment in the country, in a market sector dominated, perhaps, by one major player? How will that major player view your business and the com-petition it offers? Remember that beauty is in the eye of the beholder.

I was recently asked to value just such a company and found it a challenging exercise. While in this particular case I recog-nised that operational improvements could be made which would greatly benefit the bottom line, I was also advised that a number of competitors had approached my client with friendly buying overtures.

On further enquiry I was not surprised to find that we were quoting against these competitors in many situations and that the customers were frequently playing us off one against the other to get the best deal.

It is not an impossible exercise to guess what that competi-tion was costing everyone – that is, after all, the benefit of free enterprise and an example of market forces at work. In such a case, the value of my client's business looked a little more encouraging.

For a start, for a larger company it provided a 'bolt-on' opportunity, meaning that the buyer could simply take over the sales force, inventories and key employees and sweep the production into his own factories, saving on overheads and with a consequent sweet impact on the bottom line.

However, in this case it might mean one less competitor in the market place, enabling the trade buyer to be a little bit more robust towards his customers. The savings from this factor alone could be significant.

Even this is not the whole story. The value of my client's company might also reflect what it is worth for the major producer not to see it fall into the hands of one of the other competitors who might provide even more formidable price competition. This is not an easy valuation to call!

Franchised businesses

This is a popular way of entering business today, and is generally considered to be less of a risk for the entrepreneur because of the support and training provided by the franchisor and the use of proved marketing systems and controls.

As with any business, the value of the franchise will tend to reflect the underlying profitability and assets employed. The franchisor's charges for services and materials will be legitimate costs of the business and initial capital expense, partly perhaps in the form of a franchise fee, may have been paid.

The value of the business based on current earnings will be affected by restrictions imposed by the franchisor in the form of territorial, product or service limitations and by the cost of transferring the ownership to a new franchise holder. On the other hand, if it is a popular franchise there might be quite a turnover in such businesses and values could be well established.

Professional firms

Many professional practices such as accountants, lawyers and surveyors are conducted through partnerships, although in some cases they are now being allowed to incorporate as limited companies.

In most of these firms, the major asset consists of the partners' knowledge, skills and contacts. As they say, 'The assets go down in the lift every night'! There will be little in the way of tangible assets but there may well be a solid core of repetitive ongoing business. Think of the chartered accountant who does your annual audit, for example. Most clients rarely change auditors unless there is definite dissatisfaction with the present firm's services or charges.

Over the years, professional practices have developed performance yardsticks on their businesses, relating gross fees to normal levels of overhead and administrative costs. Profits available to the partners can be estimated with reasonable confidence, and it has become common to relate values to gross fees rather than to profits realised.

While such a valuation might be entirely appropriate for four-fifths of such businesses, if your business is much more profitable than most of your competitors, for whatever reason, you will seek a profits-based valuation. If you are not doing as well as the rest of the pack you will stick to a formula based on gross fees.

Generally, the practitioners in any profession are well aware of the accepted valuation yardsticks used and need little or no help from advisers outside their sphere of activity. As with everything else, there are exceptions.

A few years ago, we valued and sold an engineering consultancy for a consideration much greater than anything achievable on a gross fee basis. In this case, while gross fee income was considerable, almost everyone was salaried. The business had been set up as a limited company with five shareholders and most of the profits devolved to them.

Pharmaceutical companies

Businesses and products in this sector are a law unto themselves. Owing to the high profits that they have made over the years, the major pharmaceutical companies are aggressively seeking to add new products to their lines and will pay, apparently, astronomical prices for a product with potential. In some cases, I have seen valuations based on a 4, 5 or even 10 times multiple on *turnover* let alone profits. Certainly normal valuation methods are inappropriate in this sector.

Media businesses

This sector could also be considered under 'lifestyle', and it is again a playground for wealthy investors seeking primarily to extend their own personal influence in the world at large rather than looking for a profitable business as such.

They would, of course, dispute this and indeed some of the big names such as Rupert Murdoch and Robert Maxwell have made astute purchases and greatly improved the performance of many of the companies they have taken over – even if subsequent events have tarnished the image, in the case of the latter.

It remains, however, a sector that is difficult to value by conventional standards because of the non-commercial benefits or advantages offered.

Chapter 10

The Economic Background

The bigger picture

When valuing your business you must take into account the general economic background – both the scene affecting the UK, Europe and the world and that smaller scene affecting your particular industry or locale.

At the time of writing it is difficult not to be aware of the problems on the UK economic scene. We are in a sharp, deep recession and, despite optimistic government noises and encouragement, the economy shows no signs of bouncing back.

The US and Canada are experiencing a similar recession and France and Germany suffer from declining levels of trading.

This recession, or really depression, has affected most industrial sectors badly, as a glance at the daily financial news will make obvious. This stems mainly from a collapse in consumer confidence with a ripple effect spreading from the retail sector to manufacturers, producers, importers and service organisations.

We have a history in Britain of 'booms and busts'. We go on a 'borrowing binge', everyone feels better, we have 'never had it so good', and then things get out of hand. The government slams on the brakes by putting interest rates up.

As if that were not enough, the banks restrict lending and increase their margins to compensate for the inevitable 'busts'. The whole thing escalates and before long we are into a deep recession with the consequent decline in business and personal confidence.

The government accentuated this cycle in 1988 by reducing personal tax rates and signalling impending changes to mortgage deductions for tax purposes.

The impact on business values

Whatever the reason, this volatility will affect business values dramatically. The astute or lucky owner who sold out in 1988 must be satisfied with his decision today. Selling out in 1992 is a very different proposition.

The housing market offers a good analogy reflecting the swings in optimism and pessimism both tangibly and graphically. When confidence finally breaks down, as it did in 1990, not only do housing values fall severely, the volume of sales or activity drops as well. There is a reluctance to sell by owners at what they see as depressed prices, and an equal reluctance to commit by purchasers who have funds but fear that values will drop further yet.

In the case of business owners, the poor values they receive for the sale of their businesses may not be enough to help them secure a suitable retirement income. They may well decide to soldier on if they believe that the upturn in the economy is only, say, 18 months away. In my entire business career, I have never seen such a lack of business confidence as in 1992.

In fairness, entrepreneurs have good grounds for such lack of confidence. They expanded in the 1980s, urged on by an expansive government investing in new equipment, facilities and marketing – all fuelled by bank lending. As long as market demand continued or, better, expanded, everything was fine; but once business actually declined, the income generated from sales was no longer sufficient to service the debt, ie to pay back the borrowing and interest incurred. The result is a cash crisis, and since many bank loans are effectively repayable on demand, the banks can quickly put companies into receivership.

It is, indeed, a crude and highly geared system where a small loss of confidence combined with an increase in interest rates puts costs up, reduces revenue and precipitates a 20–30 per cent swing in profitability. For many smaller companies this is just too much.

In this environment the small, inadequately financed business must be more vulnerable to economic swings than the major multinationals. It is for this reason that many of the larger companies emerge stronger at the end of a recession, while a good number of small entrepreneurial players are no longer around.

In Chapter 15 we will discuss ways of holding your business together in a difficult business climate and improving the business with an eye to its eventual sale once conditions improve.

At present, many owners are recognising a decline in the value of their businesses over the last two to three years of the order of 30–50 per cent and buyers tend now to be over-pessimistic just as they were over-optimistic in 1988.

The swings in value always seem to go too far. Unless a business sale is being forced on you by death, illness or economic difficulties, however, the present drop in values may be academic.

When times are good, business people find it difficult to appreciate how well things are going. They feel all the progress being made by the business can be ascribed to their own valiant efforts and believe that growth will go onwards and upwards for ever. In this environment some buyers pay ridiculous prices for acquisitions, investing as we say in the 'chairman's ego'. These are great opportunities for realistic vendors.

There is, however, no harm in carrying out a valuation of your business at a low point in the economic cycle. For one thing, it will certainly help you to recognise improving values as the economy moves out of recession. Whether the economy is booming or in decline, however, these shifts do not affect every business or every sector equally. In a recession some gain, even if most lose, and it is now time to look at some of the differing reactions of value to economic cycles.

Factors affecting valuations

Size and strength

As we have discussed, in a difficult economy the large companies will tend to perform better because of their greater financial strengths, breadth of activities, international spread and tough effective management. We can all see that the 'alpha' stocks on the London Stock Exchange are performing well while most of the small companies have suffered significant declines in their market value over the last few years.

In addition to the inherent strength of the large companies there is also the weight of money argument. The institutions investing pension fund or insurance monies, mutual fund receipts etc must invest this, come hell or high water. It is less risky in times of recession to put it into the major companies. After all, no one was ever fired for recommending IBM.

The smaller quoted companies, however well managed, tend to be neglected during such a period and their price/ earnings multiples suffer. There is an agonising reappraisal of many of the former stock market stars with drastic results.

Since the small to medium-sized public company is normally the most likely purchaser of your business, it is easy to see why values suffer. Smaller companies are reluctant to issue shares to fund the acquisition because of the depressed price of those shares and the impact it has on the existing shareholders; ie they do not want to dilute their current shareholders' interests. If they go to their bankers for money they will probably receive a glassy-eyed stare and a rejection. The bankers, too, prefer to put their money with the big boys.

In such a scenario, therefore, where there is a perception of greater risk and a requirement for higher rates of return to compensate, these factors will push down the price that the buyer will pay for your business.

The general rule is that the stronger your company is financially, the better it will tend to hold its value, since it will be seen as more likely to emerge from the recession intact.

Fashionable activities

In recessionary climates everyone goes for businesses in defensive sectors. These are companies that have the ability to defend strongly in difficult times because they are involved in essential products or services that cannot easily be avoided or deferred.

The most obvious sectors which spring to mind include food and food processing, medical supplies and instrumentation, services related to cost control, death and taxes, and certain parts of the insurance industry, particularly companies involved in loss protection, adjusting and assessment. A debt collection agency or receivership practice would also be attractive.

For companies in such defensive sectors, a recessionary climate is a good time to raise new money. The institutions are searching for suitable investment opportunities and they will feel safer putting money into a well-financed and strong supermarket chain than they would in investing in a new manufacturing business. This is the reason why we have seen considerable investment raised recently, for instance, by the big food multiples.

Other markets

Different parts of Britain experience recession in different ways. We are all aware that the current recession has hit the south east hard but it has come much later, and perhaps more mildly, in the Midlands and the north east.

The 'thirty-somethings' in our population have been particularly hard hit during the last few years. They were achievers, starting their careers just as the economy was taking off in the early 1980s. They anticipated, with reason, drawing on their own experiences, an ever-improving economy, and spent and borrowed accordingly. Inflation would bail them out. With large mortgages and credit card debts to service, these people are now having to cut back fiercely. If your business caters primarily to this market, its value will be downgraded at present.

On the other hand, many of our senior citizens have 'never had it so good'. Higher interest rates produce increased investment income for them, while pressure on prices has held the cost of most goods fairly stable and, in some cases, even reduced them. The hobby sector, for instance, particularly that part catering largely to people in their fifties and sixties taking up, say, fine art or leisure/sports, has known no recession at all.

Specific sectors

Construction and housing

This is, of course, a diverse sector and different parts of the industry will perform in different ways. Some of those companies catering to public infrastructure which is largely funded by government, including road, rail, schools and hospitals, might do well in a recession particularly if the government is 'priming the pump', ie investing in capital projects to get the economy going.

The commercial sector will tend to reflect the general slowdown in the economy in terms of activity but since many projects have a long 'tail', in other words the actual time from conception to completion may span four or five years, the results may not be immediately obvious. We have all marvelled at the level of construction activity in the City of London at the moment, given that the demand for additional space has long since disappeared.

By contrast, the impact of confidence on the residential sector is much more quickly felt and when the house owner turns negative, not only does this hit house sales but it ricochets throughout an entire servicing sector involving furniture, carpet and appliance manufacturers, distributors and retailers, gardening suppliers, removal companies, surveyors, estate agents and so on.

Again, however, there may be parts of even this sector which may improve during such a period, including DIY and rental agencies, businesses catering to those improving their present property rather than selling, and those renting rather than buying.

Automotive

Britain has a distorted automotive industry owing to the fact that 60 per cent of all new cars are purchased by companies as employee fringe benefits. This is gradually changing as the taxation of these benefits increases, but government subsidies have created an overblown sector which is due for correction.

Motor dealers and garages are particularly vulnerable in a down-turn, given the highly capital-intensive nature of their activities, particularly those catering for the top end of the market.

Clothing and textiles

In this sector there are some excellent defensive companies like Marks and Spencer who are selling good quality everyday clothing at sensible prices. One marketing specialist I know claims that in a recession people move to quality and away from impulse buying – they want to spend their money on clothing which is going to wear well as it may be needed for quite a while! Taken in conjunction with their accent on food, Marks and Spencer must be one of the most defensive companies in the country.

The other side of this coin is represented by those suppliers and retailers catering for high fashion items. These people normally experience a severe downturn in a recession and many disappear altogether.

Catering and travel

In a recession, businesses and individuals may cut back on holidays and business travel. This was accentuated by the uncertainties created by the Gulf War and this section of the economy has still not bounced back. Customers turn to more sensibly priced hotels and restaurants in an effort to economise and, clearly, companies are cutting back on conferences and residential training courses.

Again, it is not necessarily bad news for everyone. The demise of the International Leisure Group wiped out 20–30 per cent of holiday capacity at a stroke and improved considerably the prospects of those players remaining in this market. I am also told that many people receiving redundancy settlements choose to spend them on holidays abroad before starting to search for a new position.

Conclusion

In valuing your business, it is important to be clear about your sector and its position relative to the current market.

If your business is in loss adjusting or loss assessment, it might be a marvellous time to look for a buyer; the same would apply if you had a small receivership business since most receivers are worked off their feet at present. If you are in high fashion – beware!

You might consider the perception that potential buyers will have of your business. Sometimes it is more important to position or present your business in a favoured sector or to accent specific activities undertaken in that sector.

However, we cannot get away from the fact that 80–90 per cent of businesses are being adversely affected by the current recession and all most owners can do is batten down the hatches and aim to survive until the sun comes out again! At least it is easier at such times to tighten up business practices, shed surplus staff and resist exorbitant pay demands.

The composition, as opposed to the value, of assets and liabilities will also make a difference in such an environment. A strong working capital position will help, particularly where the bulk of the liabilities is in the form of trade creditors rather than bank loans repayable on demand. In difficult times, your creditors are much more likely to go along with you and help to support your business than a bank manager who is being harried by head office to reduce lending and prone to making arbitrary decisions.

Chapter 11

Other Complications

Capital structure

I recall reading an authoritative treatise on business valuations written from the professional's point of view and was surprised at the different combinations of capital and debt structures. Reference was made not only to ordinary and preference shares but also to redeemable convertible cumulative preference stock, convertible loan, participating preferred shares, subordinated debentures and so on.

Where your company has a complicated share and debt structure, this will have an impact not just on the division of proceeds of any sale of the business between the various shareholders and classes of shareholders and lenders, but on your ability to sell at all. They may all have to be consulted. A private company is, after all, one in which the directors have the power to restrict the sale and transfer of its shares.

Apart from the possible liabilities arising from such a capital structure, which have to be satisfied first, some buyers may not want to grapple with the complexities of such an organisation or will be unwilling to incur the legal costs necessary to straighten it out, unless it is a significant acquisition for them.

If your business has such a complicated capital structure, it may not be simple to arrive at a sensible valuation unless there is some way you can enable the buyer to take over a 'clean' position. This may be done, for example, by transferring or hiving down assets to a new company prior to disposal. Throughout this book we have been talking about the purchase of 100 per cent of the business. No quoted company wants minority shareholders. This is one area where technical advice may be required.

However, on reflection, more than 90 per cent of all the

businesses we look at have just one class of shares and two or three shareholders. It follows, therefore, that most owners need not be concerned with such esoteric capital structures, however fascinating they might be to the professionals as an intellectual exercise.

Minority interests

Even if you have only one class of shares, however, you may well have an uncle with 25 per cent of the shares who can cause trouble or would not favour a sale under any circumstances, perhaps for emotional reasons.

Under the 'constitution' of most companies, referred to as the Memorandum and Articles of Association, a shareholder with less than 10 per cent of the equity has to go along with the wishes of the majority. Where dissenting shareholders own 10 per cent or more, and certainly where they own more than 25 per cent of the shares, problems can arise unless they are all agreed on what they want to achieve.

The summary on page 101 lists the significant levels of shareholdings and the implications at each level.

If the shares are widely held, there is not much sense in establishing a valuation of the company other than as a purely philosophical exercise, unless most or all of the shareholders are of a mind to contemplate selling, or a value is required for a proposed sale between them.

Where they are all likely to disagree on the future course of the company or the desirability of selling, any valuation you arrive at may prove meaningless.

When we say that the company is being valued on the basis of 100 per cent of the business, this implies that we are able to deliver 100 per cent of the shares to a buyer, by hook or by crook! Most buyers will not want to purchase a company with significant minority interests. They will generally consider the nuisance value too costly. Therefore, such a position may affect and reduce the value of the business being sold.

Other Complications – Minority Interests

Shareholdings. The impact of different levels of investment

Where the buyer does not acquire 100 per cent of the shares he has to operate the company under possible constraints imposed by the minority shareholders. The minority shareholders can claim, for instance, under certain circumstances that they are being 'oppressed' by the majority owners and can generally have a considerable nuisance value. For this reason many buyers will not consider acquiring less than 100 per cent of the shares unless they plan to leave shares with management, for example, for motivational purposes.

The impact of different percentage shareholdings or levels of investment can be summarised briefly as follows:

10%	A minority shareholder has the right to call an Extraordinary General Meeting.
20%	A 'corporate' shareholder can treat the acquisition as an associated company, ie can sweep a pro-rata share of profits into its own figures, not merely dividends paid.
25%	The minority shareholder is able to block certain actions of majority shareholders – generally those requiring a special resolution including changes in Articles or name.
51%	Majority shareholding – owner has effective control and can dismiss board of directors. Where owner is itself a company, company acquired will become a subsidiary and its accounts consolidated with parent.
75%	Significant threshold from a corporation tax point of view. Tax losses in acquired company can be offset in effect, against profits elsewhere in the group through group loss relief. Capital assets can be transferred to other companies in the group and roll-over relief is available to other group companies.
90%	Owner of 90 per cent of the shares can generally acquire the remaining 10 per cent of the shares compulsorily.
100%	Wholly owned. No minority shareholdings.

Business Expansion Scheme

Complications are also arising in some of the businesses funded through the Business Expansion Scheme. The Business Expansion Scheme is a government-approved scheme whereby people can subscribe for the shares of unquoted companies and deduct the amount invested from their taxable income in that year.

The eventual proceeds on sale of the shares are tax free in their hands, providing, in theory at least, significant potential for real capital gains. For investors to benefit, the shares must be held for five years and the investor must not participate in the running of the business or be related to the owner of the business.

Frequently, merchant banks and other financial inter-mediaries have been instrumental in assembling groups of investors to finance such companies with the intermediary often taking shares or share options as part of its remuneration package. At the end of the five-year period there is, understandably, considerable interest on the part of both the intermediary and the individual investors in selling shares and realising gains. In such situations, however, differences in outlook between owners, intermediaries and individual investors can create problems in arriving at an acceptable valuation.

Land and buildings and restrictions on use

Again we come back to that old chestnut – freehold land and buildings. Since this subject is very much tied up with the tax ramifications it will be dealt with at greater length in Chapter 14. However, we might usefully consider here the value of property with restrictions on use.

Sometimes the landlord may have stipulated that the property occupied by the business is subject to a condition that only specific types of business can be conducted from those premises.

We saw an example recently of office and warehouse accommodation rented at a peppercorn rent on just such a basis. The valuation could be built up on three different assumptions:

1. *The vendor did nothing.* In this case what is the lease worth with the restriction on use? A trade buyer intending to continue to use the site will have an advantage and may be prepared to pay for it.
2. *The vendor bought the freehold, removing the restriction.* This would deplete cash or increase borrowings with a consequent impact on interest charges. A substantial asset, however, can now be included in the balance sheet.
3. *The vendor could pay the landlord to remove the restriction.* The cost of this concession could be treated as a capital item and, perhaps, written off over the remaining period of the lease, increasing fixed costs.

The actual decision taken will depend on the relative costs of each course of action and the trade and objectives of the buyer.

Trading names

The trading name of the company may be important to the vendors and, again, for emotional reasons, or perhaps because of sound business reasons, they may be reluctant to sell the name together with the business. Where the name is well known in the market or particularly attractive or suitable for that business, a buyer would expect to acquire it. It is very much part of the goodwill.

If the purchaser has to design a new name and logo and incur considerable expense in launching and promoting this new name, perhaps losing customers in the process, he will lower his price. He will also want to satisfy himself as to exactly why this name is not available. He does not want to purchase the business and find the vendor setting up to compete against him under the old name. It may be possible to negotiate the use of that name for a transitional period of, say, two to three years to help both parties.

The same value can even attach to a well-known telephone number. A client of mine in Toronto, with a fast food delivery service, has a telephone number recognised by thousands of young people in that city. That number must represent a significant part of the value of the business.

Personal relationships

A significant asset of the business may be a profitable distributorship agreement with, say, a French supplier to act as exclusive agent and distributor in the UK. The business owner and his French supplier have known each other for many years and the agreement may be a purely informal one, not even evidenced in writing.

The key to the whole operation might be this distributorship and in valuing the business a buyer will look carefully at the relationship to gauge the likelihood of his being able to retain this agency. Although he will welcome a letter of 'comfort' from the French supplier, indicating a willingness to continue the current arrangements, this may not completely allay his fears. Depending on the supplier's relationship with the current owner, this may simply may be an accommodation to an old friend to help achieve the maximum price for his business.

Similarly, as a result of years of trading and personal relationships, a major supplier might grant considerable credit to the vendor or offer other attractive terms. In the event of a new owner taking over, the supplier might use this as an opportunity to tighten up his credit terms.

In such a case, it is not just the interest cost that is involved but the availability of replacement finance. A supplier might also demand security unavailable to the buyer or at least tie up assets that could otherwise be used elsewhere in return for continuing to supply on favourable terms.

A change in ownership in a business often provides an ideal opportunity for suppliers and customers to reassess the trading relationship and look at it in a new light freed from historical emotional ties.

Where sound commercial logic is not readily apparent in the present trading relationship, the buyer will rightly express concern and in many cases will reduce the amount he is prepared to pay to compensate for perceived risks.

Legal disputes

Where you have ongoing legal disputes these may impact on the value of the business. A letter of comfort from your lawyer may not be enough to quell a buyer's fears. After all, the lawyer is only stating an opinion, not giving a guarantee.

In such a case, when valuing the business, work out what it would cost to settle this claim in full, including all legal and interest costs, and treat the amount involved as a current liability.

Pension liabilities

We have all heard horror stories where a buyer, having acquired a company, is subsequently swamped by pension fund liabilities. Many millions of pounds can easily be involved in such a situation. These liabilities arise in connection with commitments entered into by the company to fund pension benefits payable to employees based on final salary and service formulae. Salaries have a disconcerting way of outpacing investment fund growth, involving the company in the need to make heavier and heavier contributions to secure the benefits legally payable.

Even if the company's pension plan is over-funded today, the situation can still swing into a deficit through losses in the value of the underlying assets, investment income generated, declining annuity rates etc.

Environmental concerns

Of major concern in the United States are liabilities arising from environmental factors. These can affect not only the current owners of the business but can be tracked back to the previous owners, making it next to impossible to shed such liabilities by simply selling the company.

In the EC too, business regulations are steadily becoming more onerous in response to consumer and green lobby demands. These can be seen, for example, in the requirement to upgrade hygiene standards in slaughter houses.

Actual earnings and net asset values are all very well, but if the company is facing a multi-million pound re-equipment requirement to meet new EC standards or be driven out of business, the impact of such a requirement on the value of the business and its saleability is considerable. To the extent that such expenditure cannot be offset by higher prices, the value of a company will reduce to reflect this state of affairs. This will be especially true where competitors are not in the same situation.

Tax losses

It may be difficult for a new owner to take full advantage of tax losses accruing to the business. Frequently, deriving value from these losses requires close co-operation between buyer and seller. Part of the consideration payable may well be dependent on achievement of such savings.

In preparing a valuation we have in the past put a value on tax losses of 6 per cent of their face value. In the present difficult economic climate with many companies awash with such losses, the percentage may be even lower. They will, in any case, generally only be available to a buyer continuing the same trade.

Timing

We have been talking throughout of a valuation under current conditions and in the current market. It may be, however, that owing to tax considerations, relocation plans and so on, the business is to be valued as at a future date. Where this date is no more than a few months away we can probably ignore the question of timing. It will often take three to six months to complete a sale under ideal circumstances anyway.

However, where timing constraints push the sale date further forward, many other factors come into play. Although the owner may enjoy the benefit of retirement relief for tax purposes in one year's time on achieving the age of 55, for example, by that date the business may have improved or deteriorated significantly. The tax regime may also have changed completely. We may even find, for instance, a new government elected, creating a whole new economic scenario.

Chapter 12

Pulling It All Together

Valuations based on earnings

It is time now to pull together the various calculations we have
been making, in an attempt to reach a consensus valuation –
a valuation range, in fact, which will serve as a base line or
point of reference for you in terms of your business.

We have already emphasised the importance that buyers
will place on earnings and we developed an earnings-based
valuation.

You will recall that we looked at earnings, historic, current
and projected and adjusted these to a realistic arm's-length
basis after stripping out all the perquisites and benefits
extracted by the present owners. We then multiplied these
earnings by a suitable price/earnings ratio to develop a value
for the business as a whole.

We emphasised that a carefully chosen price/earnings
multiple will reflect the relative attractiveness of this industry
sector, the cost of finance typically incurred, the general
economic level of confidence and so on. We discounted our
multiple to reflect the strengths and weaknesses of your
business compared to its publicly quoted competitor.

The resulting valuation represented one that we felt a
typical trade buyer would be comfortable with, in terms of his
own earnings performance in the market.

Perhaps a word of caution should be given here because the
choice of that price/earnings multiple or ratio is very sensitive
indeed.

If you develop a price/earnings ratio based on some of the
more exotic multiples enjoyed by the major alpha stocks, this
may give a totally misleading valuation. The larger, heavily
traded companies tend to be institutional 'darlings' and their
share prices and consequent earnings multiples have, in

effect, been bid up to rather unrealistic levels by the sheer weight of institutional money invested. There is a tremendous amount of investment available from pension funds, investment trusts, life insurance companies etc, most of which is channelled into a limited number of large public companies.

The smaller public companies, the beta and gamma stocks, are, in fact, far more likely to be the purchasers of your company since they are still very much interested in growth and, indeed, in achieving institutional status themselves. However, these stocks, precisely because they lack a sizeable institutional following at present, do not generally command the same ratings as the alpha stocks.

Do we even need to consider any other factors?

If most acquisitions are made to acquire profits or earnings and if earnings are so important to most buyers, why not stop right there? Why do we need to consider the assets that go with the business? To explain this, let us consider two companies.

Company A earns £400,000 a year before tax but has virtually no net assets – let us say £50,000. This is, we will assume, an attractive, dynamic business, tightly run, in which the financial director has done an excellent job of minimising investment in fixed assets and, indeed, in current assets by the aggressive use of trade credit etc. It has been generating good profits for years but these have been paid out by dividend, let us suppose, to the shareholders who have, by now, considerable net worth.

Company B also generates £400,000 a year pretax and is a growing and well-run business. However, in this case the owners have chosen to retain earnings in the business, reinvesting these in equipment, property and so on, while limiting the amount of money they have taken out in the form of salaries, dividends etc.

Let us assume for the sake of simplicity that both companies are equally attractive from a trading point of view, although in different sectors. Will they both command the same value in the market place?

Putting aside the moral and ethical implications, we quickly realise that, in the case of company B, should its particular industry hit a tough patch and suffer reverses or losses for a number of years, the company has significant assets against which it can borrow. It has, in short, a cushion built in to ensure that the business is able to continue satisfactorily through difficult trading circumstances until the market turns around.

In the case of company A, the owners may well be able to continue to support their business through such a recession either by limiting drawings from the business for a while or, more likely, by lending back or investing in the business to allow it to carry on. In this case, however, the business's continued viability may be dependent on the owners' willingness to support it during that difficult period.

Although the earnings may be comparable in both companies and each company may be of equal attractiveness in terms of its trading, company B, viewed on a stand-alone basis, is inherently stronger and better able to withstand market reverses than company A. It will typically command a premium from the buyer.

Indeed, if some of the assets in company B are, in fact, surplus to the business's requirements, any proposal by B's owners that cash be extracted via, say, dividends or pension contributions, will often lead the buyer to insist that the purchase price of the business be reduced pound for pound.

It is also a fact that buyers will look at the asset cover of any purchase and try to ensure that there is no dilution of asset cover in the larger business being assembled. In other words, if 70 per cent, let us say, of the current market value of the acquirer's business is represented by net tangible assets, he will prefer to see a similar percentage represented in any company purchased.

You will recall that we considered also the composition of the assets in the company being acquired. Although mathematically equivalent, a company with £1 million of net assets without any bank borrowings whatsoever will normally prove more attractive than a company with £2 million of assets subject to a bank loan of £1 million.

In the first case, the assets are free and available as security should the need arise to raise more working capital. In the second case, there is a strong possibility that the bank has already got its claws into 90 per cent of the security effectively available.

The type of assets is also important. You will recollect that Arthur Davey with his £1 million stock of motor cars purchased at competitive trade prices can realise 95 per cent of that amount virtually overnight, whereas his brother, Geoff Davey, has his £1 million tied up in plant, machinery, stocks and work in progress – a very different proposition.

Obviously, the informed buyer will prefer a transaction where he acquires both profits and significant assets to support the purchase price being paid. The market valuation will accordingly tend to reflect both these considerations.

Our pet snake

If you look at the chart on page 113, you will see an earnings-based valuation range as a horizontal band. Using the example given in Chapter 6 we derived an earnings-based valuation of £1,581,000. Accordingly, bearing in mind the relative stability of earnings, I have plotted a band ranging from £1,525,000 to £1,650,000 on the chart.

By calculating values based on the earnings of the company over four years, this band seems sufficiently wide to represent the probable range of valuations under present circumstances.

In Chapter 7 we developed a net asset value of our company at £1,170,000 accepting, of course, that one or two of the values of particular assets could be a little out.

The underlying net asset value of a company will tend to increase year by year as profits are realised and retained in the business and, for the purposes of the illustration, a diagonal band is shown to represent different net asset values of the company. A somewhat narrower band is provided in this case, since we felt that the net asset values developed had a high probability of accuracy.

The values cross, or intercept, between £1,500,000 and £1,700,000. If our basic assumptions and calculations are reasonable, this suggests a high degree of confidence in the

Our Pet Snake

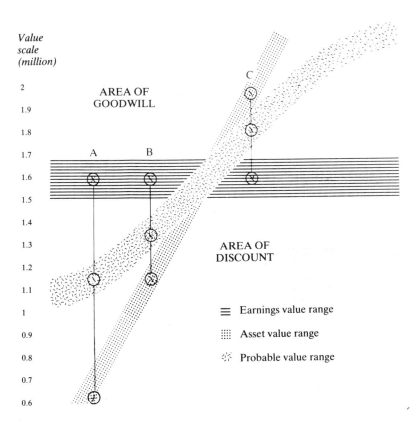

Value
scale
(million)

AREA OF
GOODWILL

AREA OF
DISCOUNT

≡ Earnings value range

⣿ Asset value range

✷ Probable value range

Plotting (three examples)

A. Business with net assets of, say, £600,000
B. Business as described in the text with net assets of £1,170,000
C. Business with net assets of, say, £2 million

value of the company for those profits where the net assets are worth, say, £1.5 million.

There is often no such match and if we plot the actual value used in Chapter 7 for net assets, calculated at £1,170,000, this falls well below the earnings valuation line. In this situation and indeed in most situations where the net asset value is less than the earnings values calculated, the likely value of the company will be dragged down somewhat to reflect the higher risk. There are less assets backing up the buyer's investment.

However, the market valuation of the business will not normally decline on a straight line basis to the net assets available because this would ignore the value of the earnings stream. The 'snake' drawn through the chart is an attempt to depict the sort of trade-off that a buyer will typically, if unconsciously, make when faced with this problem.

Where asset values exceed values based on earnings, there is a similar trade-off. In this case, the buyer may conclude that the assets are not being fully used and may not be prepared to pay full price for them.

From the chart, therefore, you can see a snake emerging: a band suggesting the probable market price this company would command at different levels of asset cover compared to a fixed earnings position. In the chart a composite value of perhaps £1,350,000 is suggested. This is a crude but useful concept, but there are one or two more considerations to bear in mind.

Where the assets are very liquid, let us say Arthur Davey's motor cars, the snake will follow net asset value fairly closely. In many cases, the profits generated from this type of activity will be more a reflection of the proprietor's skills, or his fast talking, than the inherent worth or value of the business as a system.

On the other hand, Geoff Davey's business will have a snake more along the lines of the illustration since here, with a combination of plant, equipment, trading practices etc, there should be an underlying value to the business as a whole and a better chance that the profit levels can be maintained under a new owner.

The value of an image

The image of a snake as shown is a useful one to bear in mind when valuing your business. It is, of course, only a crude depiction of real life and is certainly no better than the assumptions you have put into the formula. However, it is useful in helping to suggest where the range of values for your business lies.

Remember that everything is constantly moving: sales, profits, prospects, asset values, interest rates, competition etc, all of which will affect value. On balance, a well-designed price/earnings multiple, particularly one updated periodically to reflect the current situation, will do much to reflect at least the external influences on the business's value.

Unfortunately, it is difficult to measure the value of intangibles where these are not already coming through in terms of earnings. The business may have significant potential based on new products and development, new patents secured or new distribution agreements signed, but until these actually produce tangible benefits it is virtually impossible to reflect them in any formula. However, we are trying to establish a base line valuation here. Such intangible assets should certainly not normally detract from such a value.

Are there any other yardsticks we can use to check these valuations?

I believe there are two other yardsticks that you could consider as a check on the valuations developed above. One would be used by the larger corporate acquirers; the other is more typical of those employed by thrusting young entrepreneurs who might also be interested in purchasing your business.

1. Hurdling

Remember that it is the buyer who makes the running. Many large corporate buyers look for a minimum rate of return or cash flow on any new investment. This could be, typically, an investment in sophisticated electronic equipment to improve efficiencies in an existing production line, or an investment in additional machines.

Before considering an acquisition seriously, the buyer may require it to pass a rate of return or 'hurdle' rate in terms of profits or cash generated by the investment involved.

The hurdle rate used will reflect both the dearth or wealth of alternative investment opportunities available to that buyer and also his cost of finance. The more opportunities available to him, the higher the hurdle rate.

It is a device that the buyer will use to screen out less attractive investments. In the case of an acquisition, he must consider not only the price paid for the business, but also any additional investment required and the cost of integrating it into his present operations.

A recent survey of large US corporations indicated an average 17.2 per cent hurdle rate on all new investments. If we assume that UK borrowing costs have historically been 3–4 per cent higher than the US, this indicates a hurdle rate in the UK of at least 20 per cent. My experience is that most large UK buyers will seek a 20–25 per cent return, pretax.

Venture capitalists, of course, investing in new and high-risk green-field projects, may set a hurdle rate of 30–40 per cent – something that brings gasps of disbelief from entrepreneurs. A cautious Japanese buyer with a lower cost of capital, and a captive demand, might accept a lower rate of return.

When considering purchasing your company the buyer will project earnings ahead to make sure the investment will pass his own hurdle rate.

Taking the example above:

	£
Maintainable average pretax profits	400,000
Seller's price expectation	1,557,600
Rate of return	25%

If the buyer accepts your assumptions and projections, this will provide him with a rate of return of at least 25 per cent. If his hurdle rate is, say, 20 per cent he will certainly be prepared to look more closely at this opportunity, all other aspects being favourable.

Let us assume he has a minimum hurdle rate of 20 per cent, however, and your company produced earnings of £300,000 per annum. This would fall below his required rate of return and he might either suggest a lower purchase price or move on to consider alternative projects.

You would think that hurdle rates vary widely as bank interest rates rise and fall. In fact, these rates tend to be relatively stable and in my experience do not vary widely from one company to another in the same industry sector. The rates adopted internally by companies seem to be more influenced by the choice and availability of projects than by the cost of finance as such.

It is difficult to see why hurdle rates should not decline when interest rates are low and rise when interest rates increase. It has been suggested, however, that when interest rates are low it is generally a signal that the government are trying to stimulate a depressed or lagging economy, ie one operating at a low level and with a depressed outlook.

This could mean that, although the interest component of the hurdle rate is low, the buyer perceives a higher than normal risk factor in any new investments at that time. Perhaps he incurs the costs but the economy does not recover and it takes longer than expected to break even. He may look for a higher hurdle rate to compensate for such uncertainties.

When interest rates are at record highs, it is often because the whole economy is heating up and governments are trying to cool things. However, to the man in the street everything still looks rosy and most of us never foresee the fall off the cliff. We tend to be grateful that the economy is booming, enabling us to cover up previous errors of business judgement. In typical fashion we all feel the present boom will persist and view the risks on a new project as relatively low. At heart we are all eternal optimists.

Bearing in mind this yardstick, a required rate of return of between, say, 20–25 per cent per annum is the norm. If you are seeking a value for your company in excess of this, there has to be something very special, or attractive, or niche, about it to justify a higher price. In general terms, the number of buyers interested in pursuing such an acquisition will drop off dramatically unless they are convinced that they can significantly improve the profits.

2. Goodwill (badwill?) calculations

A number of successful entrepreneurs use yet another yardstick when valuing acquisition opportunities. They will value a company at net asset value plus or minus a goodwill factor based on the level of pretax profits experienced.

Their calculation of goodwill will be based on the ability of the business to generate a return over and above the 'pure' borrowing costs associated with the investment – a super profit. As an example:

	£
Average maintainable profits pretax pa	400,000
Net asset value	1,170,000
Associated borrowing costs at, say, 15% pa	175,000
Superprofits (£400,000 −£175,000) =	225,000
Goodwill at 1.5 × superprofits	337,500
Goodwill at 2 × superprofits	450,000
Business value at 1.5 × superprofits	
(£1,170,000 + £337,500) =	1,507,500
Value at 2 × superprofits	
(£1,170,000 + £450,000) =	1,620,000

This all looks pretty reasonable in comparison to the valuations we have developed above, but what happens when the company makes no profit or, worse still, goes into loss?

Let us consider another example:

	£
Average maintainable profits pretax pa	Break even
Net asset value	1,170,000
Associated borrowing costs at, say, 15% pa	175,000
Superprofits (losses)	(175,000)
Goodwill at 1.5 × superprofits	
(£1,170,000 − £262,500)	907,500
Goodwill at 2 × superprofits	
(£1,170,000 −£350,000)	820,000

The buyer in this case will argue that there is no way he can afford to pay net asset value for a company that is making no profit. By financing this through his bankers, by the time he has paid his borrowing costs he will actually be £175,000 per annum 'underwater'. This is apart from the costs of rationalising and improving the company's operation to make an acceptable return on the investment. He may estimate that it will take 18 months and cost £262,500 in extraordinary costs, profits forgone or interest paid, to put things on to a profitable footing. In such circumstances, he is discounting his offer for the business by a similar amount.

This will strike sellers as unduly harsh but, in fact, in an uncertain and high-risk world it is not an unreasonable position to take.

It is easy to see that, where the company is actually incurring losses, this valuation formula will savagely reduce the price a buyer is prepared to pay.

Conclusion

In this chapter we have introduced the concept of a valuation 'snake' to reconcile the differences between valuations based on earnings and assets. While this is a useful, if crude, tool for use in valuing your company it cannot really cope with significant intangible assets unless these are showing through demonstrably in earnings. These have to be subject to a judgement call.

We have also suggested two other yardsticks that may be employed by the large corporate buyer and by the thrusting entrepreneur interested in purchasing your business. There are, of course, many variants on these and each buyer will tend to have his own favourites. However, familiarity with some of the basic tools of the trade will help to demystify the valuation process.

I suggest that for many businesses a combination of these methods will produce an acceptable base line valuation and will provide a degree of confidence in responding to enquirers or considering offers received out of the blue.

Chapter 13

How Do You Get Paid?

Introduction

In Chapter 4 we described the valuation that we were seeking as one that could be expressed as net present cash. However, in many transactions the consideration will not be paid wholly in cash at completion.

The purpose of this chapter is to discuss the different forms this consideration can take and suggest ways in which these might affect the overall valuation. It will also enable you to compare offers actually received to your base line valuation.

Consideration might take other forms because of:

1. Tax considerations on the part of either the buyer or seller.
2. A desire by the buyer to encourage the vendor to maximise post-acquisition profits or performance of the acquired company by linking part of the consideration to future performance.
3. The buyer's inability to meet the full purchase price at completion.

Jam today or jam tomorrow

The different forms of consideration can be initially categorised as consideration immediately payable or consideration payable in the future – jam today or jam tomorrow.

1. *Immediate consideration.* This can take the form of cash, loan notes, pension plan contributions, golden handshakes and other forms of financial accommodation. In all these cases the cash value of the benefit conferred is easily measurable. However, a public company may offer its own shares as part of the immediate consideration payable.

The valuation of these shares may not be so straightforward.

2. *Future consideration*. This can take the form of future payments defined as to amount and timing. Alternatively, the deferred consideration may be contingent and depend, for example, on future performance of the acquired company.

   The big concern here is the strength of the 'covenant' or undertaking on the part of the buyer to support such promises. Will he be able to pay up when the deferred amount becomes due? If a bank guarantee is provided, for instance, the problem remaining is one of calculating a present cash value.

As a guiding principle in this area, most sellers seek to receive cash, or cash equivalent, for a value at least equal to the net tangible value of the business being sold or assets transferred. They will view deferred consideration as essentially 'icing on the cake'.

Let us look in more detail at the valuation of shares offered as part of the deal.

Should you accept shares?

In this case, it is usually a publicly quoted company which is making the acquisition and offering its own shares as part of the consideration to the vendor.

Where these shares can be quickly and readily sold on the market, without significantly affecting the present share price, there is no question that full value is received. But what about shares in a small quoted company where any attempt to sell more than, say, 10,000 shares a week would drive down the price?

To prevent just this catastrophe, buyers will often insert a clause in the sales contract restricting any sale of shares by the vendor for, say, two years. Effectively, you are 'locked in'.

What is the valuation of the consideration received in this case? It is certainly not equal to the present quoted value of those shares on the Stock Exchange, since they cannot be sold at that price.

Where the buyer is a publicly quoted company with a good reputation or 'following' among institutional investors, cash can often be raised through a 'vendor placing'. This is, in effect, an issue of shares made by the buying company to finance the acquisition which is 'placed' or sold on immediately by the vendor to institutions or other large investors. The proceeds are paid over to the vendors becoming, of course, cash in their hands. The institution is able to acquire a reasonable stake in the quoted company without disturbing the general market for the shares and often at a small discount.

In many cases you will be selling your company to realise cash and diversify your investment – in short, to lock in a gain and to make sure that all your eggs are not in one basket. There seems to be no point to this if the end result is that you receive a large block of shares in a small publicly quoted company run by someone else. You will not have achieved the diversification or the security you were searching for.

The use of shares can give rise to some questionable valuations. Consider the following imaginary, but not untypical, item in the financial press during 1990.

Parkridge Group plc purchases Oaklabel Limited for £8.6 million

Stanley Goldforth, Chairman of Parkridge Group plc, has announced the purchase of Oaklabel Limited for £8.6 million.

Of this consideration, £1.9 million is payable at completion in cash. The balance of the consideration, which will be calculated by reference to the profits achieved by Oaklabel over the next three years, will be satisfied in Parkridge shares.

Let us assume again, not untypically, that Parkridge itself was placed in receivership within 12 months of acquisition.

What was the real value of this business? It appears that this was represented, in effect, by cash only, because the seller presumably did not have an opportunity to sell his shares before the buyer was put into receivership.

A double whammy

One sale we negotiated a few years ago was an interesting one from this point of view and it introduced what Americans call a 'double whammy'.

The buyer was a small publicly quoted company which purchased the shares of our client partly for cash and partly on a deferred basis. Our client's business was of reasonable size compared to that of the acquiring company, and a good performance in the new business could have a significant impact on the parent's results.

Recognising these possibilities, the vendor was offered immediate cash consideration together with an earnout calculated by reference to post-acquisition profits. The earnout amount was to be satisfied in shares of the parent at 90 per cent of the average quoted price of those shares in the 30 days immediately before the expiry of the earnout period.

The business did very well and generated considerable profits within the new organisation. The result was that our vendor became a major shareholder in the public company. In fact, he gained in two ways.

As a result of the good profits, a substantial earnout amount was payable under the formula. This in turn purchased a large number of shares because the share price had slipped in the meantime.

Incidentally, in that case we also took the precaution of stipulating that, should the buyer itself be taken over prior to the completion of the earnout period, a minimum amount of deferred consideration was immediately payable in cash. All in all, the vendor did pretty well.

Deferred consideration – buyouts and earnouts

This consideration may either be definite as to amount and timing – a buyout; or contingent on future trading results (or, indeed, on some other agreed criterion) – an earnout.

Where consideration is deferred and there is *any* possibility that the buyer may not have the funds, you should insist that this payment be guaranteed by a reputable bank. If a commercial rate of interest is to be calculated and included, the amount of the deferred payment is indeed a 'present cash equivalent'. If no interest is payable, the future proceeds must be 'discounted back' to calculate the real present value. This will reflect, in effect, the interest you have lost or forgone by not having the use of those funds at completion.

An illustration of an earnout

A better price may be achievable where you are prepared to base part of the consideration on future earnings – in other words, where you will accept an earnout.

Let us look at a typical earnout agreement.

Your adjusted profits have averaged £400,000 pretax (£268,000 after tax) to the date of sale, and the asset base has been calculated at, say, £1,170,000.

The buyer concedes an earnings multiple of 5.9 times and offers £1,200,000 in cash as immediate consideration and a final payment three years later equal to 5.9 times average annual profits for the three years following acquisition less the amount of immediate consideration paid. He stipulates that final payment cannot exceed £750,000; that is, he 'caps' the final payment.

Assume profits are as follows:

	£
Year 1	390,000 pretax
Year 2	440,000 pretax
Year 3	460,000 pretax
	1,290,000

Average profits will be	£430,000 pretax
Average profits will be	£288,000 post tax @ 33%
Total consideration will be 5.9 × £288,000 or	£1,700,000
Less immediate consideration	£1,200,000
Amount of deferred consideration	£500,000

For tax reasons you will normally want to receive this deferred consideration in shares or loan notes.

Earnout pitfalls

A successful deferred earnout formula is dependent on:

1. The ability of the business and its current managers to trade profitably or fulfil the agreed conditions in the post-acquisition period. In some cases survival is enough.
2. The continued health, or at least survival, of the purchasing company and its ability to deliver at the end of the earnout period.
3. The willingness of the new owners to account equitably for the earnings of the business acquired. Parent companies sometimes have funny notions about the appropriate level of management charges.
4. The parent agreeing to maintain the acquired business as a separate accounting entity for the period of the earnout. This may pose unacceptable restraints on management's ability to manage.

Earnout formulae have to be carefully drawn up if misunderstandings are to be avoided. The treatment of issues such as research and development, capital expenditure, your management salaries and the basis and rates of interest charged, must all be addressed. A detailed business plan carefully drawn up and agreed between the parties beforehand is almost essential. Many earnouts end in tears as a result of changing circumstances or objectives.

As with a buyout, it is vital that the purchaser has the financial strength to meet earnout liabilities as they fall due. This is by no means a theoretical concern and a number of acquisitions in the advertising and public relations sectors have succeeded in generating the required post-acquisition profits only to find that their new parent can no longer raise the cash to meet its obligations. In such cases, some vendors have wisely reserved the right in the sales contract to buy back the business.

Chapter 14

Tax Considerations

Introduction

The whole subject of tax planning on the sale of the business, from the viewpoints of both vendor and purchaser, has been exhaustively discussed in a number of other publications. I am not a tax specialist and it is not my intention to write yet another tax treatise on this subject. However, a 'broad brush' introduction to the principal tax considerations is important to give you a feel for the major areas of potential and concern.

For most readers these notes will be sufficient, at this stage, to stimulate interest in the key areas for future tax planning, and should help to identify topics of personal interest to discuss with your own tax accountants. Even though a sale of the business may well be a few years away, it is never too early to start planning for such an event. However, remember that tax rules can and will change so you have to remain fairly flexible and open at this stage.

Most of the comments which follow relate primarily to incorporated businesses, ie limited companies, since, in my experience, not many businesses of any size are carried on as sole traders today – unless they are professionals constrained by their Institute.

The after-tax proceeds

In valuing the business, the real consideration to the vendor is not the gross sales price achieved but the amount that you are able to retain after tax. In my experience, many owners are devastated when they start to calculate how much of the sale proceeds will be absorbed by tax. Frequently, as a result of this discovery, they decide to soldier on.

Having a shrewd idea of the net proceeds you are likely to receive *before* entering into discussions helps to evaluate any offers received with more realism. It helps you to decide on the minimum value acceptable if the capital remaining is to provide a viable income for your later years.

In addition, not only will it alert you to ways of maximising your after-tax position, it will also indicate savings or benefits which might be available to the buyer – savings that can often be translated into securing a better offer on his part. If you let him know that you are aware of the benefits available to him, this can often be used effectively to negotiate a better deal. It is even more exciting if you can reveal to him tax planning benefits that he was not aware of.

A word of caution, however, on the subject of tax planning. More than any other area in this book, this is one for very specific advice relative to your own personal situation and circumstances. Tax rulings and decisions often seem capricious and illogical and it is fatal to act before considering all the ramifications. Bearing in mind the ideas which follow should help, however, when talking to your tax adviser to ensure that he, at least, considers the obvious areas of tax planning on your behalf.

Your personal tax position

Most owner/shareholders who read this book will have been born and will have lived most of their life in the UK. In technical terms they are 'deemed to be ordinarily resident and domiciled' in the UK and probably intend to retire here. They are involved in a business and own shares in that business either directly or indirectly through, say, a holding company.

A minority of readers will not be ordinarily resident or domiciled in the UK. Although they may have been born here, they may have lived abroad for many years and intend to retire there, in perhaps a warmer climate. For such readers, there may be additional scope for tax saving, which is not available to the rest of us, and that possibility will certainly exercise the ingenuity of their advisers.

In addition, some UK residents will have had the foresight, in years gone by, to ensure that the shares in their company are held by an offshore vehicle – ie a holding company or 'freezer' trust or some such combination. In this instance, their direct interests relate to, say, a trust rather than to shares in the UK company itself. They will have set up these arrangements years ago when the business may have had little or no real value.

In such cases, the bulk of this chapter will not unduly concern them, since any capital gains on the sale of shares will not attract tax immediately in the UK. Tax will, however, generally be payable on money remitted to the UK.

The 1991 Budget tightened up considerably on the attractions offered by offshore trusts. If your arrangements were not already in place on 17 March 1991, however, it is probably too late now to do anything. A detailed discussion on the taxation of offshore trusts is obviously outside the scope of this book.

Types of taxes payable

There are four different taxes payable on the sale of a business or assets. These are:

1. *Value added tax and 2. Stamp duty*

These are relatively small areas of concern in the overall picture except perhaps on the sale of the assets rather than shares. However, a competent chartered accountant should be able to help you minimise your liabilities to such charges before the final transaction is completed.

3. *Capital gains tax*

This is a tax levied on the owner or shareholder following the sale of shares in his company, at a value in excess of the cost of those shares, after allowing for indexation for inflation. Such gains will be included in your taxable income in the year of sale and will be subject to normal personal rates of income tax. Ways of deferring or minimising such capital gains will be dealt with later in this chapter.

A sole trader selling assets at a profit will be similarly treated.

4. Corporation tax

This tax will be borne by your company on the profits realised on the sale of assets. The profits made will simply be added to the company's taxable income, increasing the corporation tax payable in that year.

Any additional liability to tax, of course, reduces the value of the net tangible assets in the company and perhaps the value of the company. It follows that if the shareholders subsequently sell the shares of the company they may, in effect, be taxed twice on profits – once when key assets are sold by the company and again when the shares of the company themselves are sold. Not an attractive prospect!

Capital gains tax

Capital gains tax (CGT) comes into play when you sell shares in a company for a price, or consideration, that is greater than a base cost established by the Inland Revenue. This base cost is the cost or value of those shares as at 31 March 1982, increased by an allowance for inflation, calculated on a monthly basis, to the date of sale. Ever helpful, the Inland Revenue publish an Indexation Allowance Chart to enable you to calculate the current base cost. If additional capital has been contributed to the company in the interim period, this will be taken into account and indexed also from the date on which that capital was introduced.

A capital gain arises when the shares are sold at a value greater than the current indexed base cost. This gain will be added to your personal income for tax purposes in the *year of sale*. In most cases it will, therefore, attract tax at your top marginal rate – 40 per cent at present.

Historically, capital gains were taxed at a lower rate than personal income tax rates but this is not true at present. There is always the possibility that capital gains tax rates will be reduced in future, but it is more likely that capital gains tax rates will remain at 40 per cent with personal income tax rates tending to increase. This would re-create the need to distinguish carefully between gains from income and capital – something we have moved away from in recent years.

Either way, a sale of the shares of the company has no impact on the company's own tax liabilities and position.

Corporation tax

Where the company itself sells assets, any gain realised over the value of those assets, as assessed by the taxman, will be swept into normal trading profits and attract corporation tax at the appropriate rates – normally 33 or 25 per cent for small companies.

In effect, by selling assets the company is converting assets from one form, eg plant and machinery, into another form, eg cash.

In determining taxable gains on the sale of assets, the Inland Revenue use their own depreciation rules, disregarding the company's depreciation calculations. They grant capital allowances (depreciation) on most assets, including certain additions to property, plant and equipment, motor vehicles etc, and industrial building allowances for certain classes of buildings. These allowances are used to reduce the value of the assets for tax purposes. Where a profit is realised on the sale of assets, following the taxman's own calculations, this profit, or balancing charge as it is called, is effectively added to the taxable income of the company for that year.

Minimising capital gains tax on the sale of shares

It will be seen that we are primarily concerned with your liability to capital gains tax on the sale of shares of the business and it is now time to look at the various reliefs available to minimise this tax.

It may be, of course, that there is no capital gain on the sale of the company. Where the performance of the business has been relatively pedestrian over the last few years, or where most of the profit has already been extracted in one form or another, the sale proceeds may be less than the indexed base cost.

Assuming, however, that your years of effort have been well rewarded, let us look at the various reliefs available to you.

Retirement relief

This is available to the owners or active shareholders of the company provided that they have attained the age of 55 and have spent ten years or more working in the business. It is a personal relief available to both husband and wife in defined circumstances where they are selling the whole, or certainly the major part, of the business. Surprisingly, they can even accept employment with the new owners if they so wish after retirement.

The retirement relief grants complete exemption to capital gains on the first £150,000 each and 50 per cent of the gain on the excess over that up to the next £450,000 each. This relief is only available for assets actively used in the business, ie quoted investments would be excluded.

Pension contributions

The owners can draw additional remuneration from the company and make contributions to their personal pension plans prior to sale. Alternatively, the company can make contributions to corporate plans to the extent that the current legislation allows. This has the effect of deferring or 'sheltering' tax on those contributions but does, of course, reduce the asset value of the business being sold by the net after-tax amount. It will normally reduce the consideration that will be paid by the buyer.

Although you may be able to borrow against pension plans and although part of your pension fund may be commutable tax free into cash at retirement, it is still possible to go completely overboard on pension contributions. It may be better to pay 40 per cent tax now to release some funds immediately. Only time will tell.

Other benefits

There is nothing to prevent you increasing your remuneration from the business in the year prior to sale but this will, of course, attract tax in the normal way. For this purpose a dividend would look better in the accounts than excessive salaries, bonuses or expenses.

Distribution of shares

It is possible in the years prior to sale to spread the shares in the company around the family, giving or selling them to sons, daughters, uncles and aunts and so on. However, disposals to other family members are taxable in their hands. An election can be made for hold-over relief on the gift of business assets or shares as long as this is jointly claimed by both donor and recipient. But remember, you are, in effect, giving value away. This may, of course, reduce not only your own potential liability to capital gains tax but may also reduce total potential liability for the family. However, such action can bring many other problems in its wake and is not something to be undertaken lightly or without careful thought and planning.

Golden handshakes

Where the owner and/or his wife decide to accept employment with the new owners of their company, it is possible, a year or two later, for them to receive tax-free golden handshakes on finally retiring from the business. However, this must not be an explicit or contractual undertaking reached at the time of the sale. A golden handshake can be worth up to £30,000 each free of all taxes.

Pre-sale dividends

Where the company being sold has significant retained earnings or revenue reserves, a cash or stock dividend can be declared prior to sale. This can effectively reduce the tax borne by the vendor from a maximum of 40 per cent to 20 per cent on the gross amount of the dividend received. If you believe this might be applicable in your case, ask your accountant to do the calculations for you. The purchaser is unlikely to complain – it can be easier for him to finance.

Roll-over relief

If ICI or Shell is buying your business, maybe you can persuade them to settle in shares rather than in cash. No capital gains tax will be payable until the shares received are themselves sold at a later date. In the event that part of the consideration is settled in shares, the capital gains will be similarly pro-rated.

If the shares in your company are widely held throughout your large family, a few shares can be sold each year, by each of your relatives, to take advantage of the annual capital gain exemption (currently £5800). If you have a capital gain 'exposure' of £1 million, however, it will take quite a while, unless you have a very large family. Here again, relief is not automatic and your accountant will have to follow the necessary approvals and procedures to the letter.

In your desire to minimise immediate taxes, however, do not accept shares that could become worthless in future or where there is a high degree of risk attaching to their present value. The stock market is a volatile place – some would call it a casino!

Unless you would be prepared to invest heavily in the buying company because of its intrinsic merits, you should not consider taking more than a small proportion of the consideration in shares.

The number of vendors who take shares in a speculative, 'thinly capitalised' company is surprising. They swap the security of a business they own 100 per cent for shares in a company controlled by someone else who may well be considerably more cavalier. In difficult times many of these small companies can suffer horrendously or even disappear without trace.

This is a good example of not allowing tax considerations to override the commercial logic of your decision.

Convertible loan notes

You might ask the buyer to settle part of the price with convertible loan notes instead of paying in cash. In effect, you agree to give a loan to the company with options to redeem this loan for cash at a future date or dates. You may also get interest in the meantime.

This may help the buyer to finance the transaction and will defer the payment of capital gains tax on the sale into future years. The principle here is not to accept loan notes from anyone other than an ICI or Shell unless you are getting those notes fully guaranteed by a reputable bank.

Deferred payments

As we saw in previous chapters, for sound commercial reasons a buyer will often offer you deferred consideration as part of the total transaction package. This consideration can be definite in amount and timing (a buyout) or can be contingent on future performance (an earnout). It is not normally an arrangement that you will initially recommend to the buyer but it may well have the double benefit of enabling him to finance a larger purchase and enabling you to defer capital gains tax on part of the consideration until a later date.

If you are optimistic regarding the company's future prospects and profitability but cannot wholly convince the buyer, this might be an appropriate negotiating point.

Where the buyer suggests an earnout, he is generally making this offer to provide you with a healthy 'carrot' or incentive to make sure that you stay committed to the success of the business while he is getting his own people firmly into the saddle. It may be, however, that he cannot afford to pay the full amount immediately.

In either case, apart from the commercial considerations, make sure that the buyer can afford to meet the deferred payments, by securing some form of bank guarantee or cross-guarantee from his other companies. In addition, be careful to make sure that there are no tax 'time-bombs' in the arrangements.

Unless you agree to take the deferred consideration in the form of shares or convertible loan notes, you could face a demand from the Inland Revenue for payment of capital gains tax based on the full consideration, including the deferred portion, now, while you are not going to receive a considerable part of the proceeds for perhaps two to three years, if at all. Make sure that your friendly accountant covers this one.

Where the company sells assets

In the previous section we considered carefully the tax implications of selling shares. What about the situation where your company itself sells assets instead? Let us look at an example first.

Let us assume that you have shares in a company whose single largest asset is an investment in freehold land and buildings. These are carried at original 1935 costs in the books and are worth substantially more today than when purchased 50 odd years ago. Sale of that land and buildings will trigger substantial capital gain taxes. What is more, you may have an emotional attachment to the property, would like to keep it in the family and calculate that it would generate a useful retirement income in its own right.

You have two choices. In the first case, you can set up a new company, a simple exercise, and transfer all the business assets into the new company, leaving only the land and buildings in the old company. You can do this by allocating a proportionate number of shares in the new company to old company shareholders.

You can then agree to sell all the shares of the new company, triggering possible capital gains, as described in the previous section, in the hands of the owners and shareholders in respect of gains on the sale of the business. The owners keep shares in the company owning the freehold property, still sitting in there at a 1935 cost.

One advantage to the buyer in this case is that he can acquire a clean company and make sure that any skeletons in the cupboard will remain with the vendors. This should make the job of agreeing warranties and undertakings that much simpler.

The alternative course is for the company itself to sell those business assets and liabilities as a package to the purchaser. As we have seen before, this triggers off slightly different results. The gains realised on the sale of the assets now become profits in the company and the company will pay corporation tax on these gains in the normal course. It is possible, however, to declare a dividend and transfer the liability for taxes effectively to the shareholders. The course chosen will depend on the exact circumstances of each case.

To defer tax, it is also possible to reinvest, within a defined period of time, the proceeds of the sale of the assets into other trading assets. For instance, your company could sell its plant, materials, equipment, goodwill and so on, for cash, investing the proceeds in the purchase of other equipment which could be rented out to provide an income stream. This is another version of the 'roll-over' reliefs referred to above. Indeed, the company could sell the business assets for shares in the purchasing company and defer capital gains until those shares are eventually sold.

A sole trader has similar roll-over options available to defer payment of capital gains taxes.

In the event that the transaction is a mix of cash, shares and perhaps other securities such as loan notes, the capital gains will be pro-rated accordingly for tax purposes.

In the examples quoted, the basic activities or trade of your company may have changed but the company carries on.

There is, however, a whole set of taxation rules relating to the cessation of business where your company stops trading. Where, however, as in the above example, the nature of the trade changes from perhaps manufacturing to property rental, the major concern might be the difficulty of setting off trading losses for tax purposes against future profits.

The position of the buyer

A buyer, generally, will prefer to purchase specific assets and assume specific liabilities. The transaction will be simpler and there will be flexibility in the allocation of the purchase price to the assets acquired. This gives considerable scope for ensuring that the bulk of expenditure is related to assets for which capital allowances are available.

This could, in turn, create a conflict with the requirements of the seller who might prefer a different allocation of the sale proceeds. In such cases the buyer and seller, or more likely their advisers, must get together and agree on a common position.

Other points to watch

It may seem premature to consider these at the time of carrying out a valuation but there are a number of other pitfalls which you should bear in mind.

1. Timing of the sale: since capital gains tax is paid on 1 December in the tax year following the tax year in which the disposal occurs, there is an obvious timing advantage to completing the sale of a company after 5 April. This buys you an additional year to meet the tax bill.
2. A vendor may personally own freehold property which is essential to the business. This property can be injected into the company ahead of the sale to realise a better price. The sale of the property into the company at current market value may create a capital gain in the hands of the vendor.

   This is acceptable as long as the sale of the company actually does go through and provided that the proceeds received are sufficient to pay the capital gains tax on both property and business. If a large part of the consideration is deferred, however, tax might become payable before the vendor receives the funds.
3. The payment of a stock dividend to minimise the vendor's total tax bill must be made before completing the sale of the company. If, for any reason, the sale does not go

through the shareholders may be faced with a large tax bill and no funds to pay it.

4. Throughout this chapter we have assumed that the company is being sold for *bona fide* commercial reasons. Where there is any suggestion at all that the sale is being effected for purely tax reasons, the Inland Revenue can take a very different position. It is for this reason that prior clearance is sought from the Inland Revenue for the proposed transaction.

Conclusion

As part of an exercise to value your company, you must be aware of the likely current tax ramifications upon sale and the impact that these might have on the net funds available to you. Recognising the major reliefs and pitfalls ahead will suggest specific actions that might be taken as part of any 'grooming for sale' exercise.

Chapter 15

Grooming the Business for Sale

Maximising the benefit

The sale of your business may represent the summation of a life's work. Ideally, it should provide a pension plan for your later years, a 'pot of gold', or a return for those ten or twenty years of effort.

Whether or not you have built a company from scratch over the years, you will wish to maximise the benefits realised from the sale, both in terms of the actual price realised and also in terms of the amount you are able to retain on an after-tax basis.

You may be perceptive and opportunistic, selling your company at an advantageous time and some owners do seem to have a good feel for such an opening. On the other hand, you could be unfortunate and face a forced sale because of ill health, family commitments, divorce or other personal difficulties.

It is always sad to see a lifetime's work sold off by the receiver for a derisory amount. Such a sale represents both a real and an emotional loss to the owner of the company. Timing of the sale, therefore, assumes critical importance.

Wherever possible, you must plan ahead, especially if you have thoughts of selling in a few years' time, either to retire or take on a second career. The old Boy Scouts' motto 'Be Prepared' is still very apt.

In this case, the objective of planning ahead is to be able to shape or groom your company over the next few years to put it into the best possible position, so that when you decide to sell, or when an opportunity for sale arises, your chances of getting a good price are improved.

General pointers to bear in mind

Some of the ideas I am about to suggest have been encountered earlier in this book. They are all, however, points that should improve the attractiveness of your company to a buyer and deserve such re-emphasis.

Improving operational effectiveness

Whether or not you are contemplating a sale in the near future, you should obviously put the business on to the best possible financial footing. This means sensible cost controls, maximising market opportunities, optimising price/volume trade-offs, eliminating waste, exercising strong cash control etc. This is good business practice at any time, but is of particular value when a sale is contemplated.

In a private company you can manage the business for the benefit of the family shareholders. If the future for this business in your family stretches out to eternity, because you have a number of capable sons and daughters to take over, reported profits may be less important than the lifestyle afforded to the family by the business.

Where, however, an 'exit' is in prospect, even if this is three or four years away, you need to give thought now to the shape the business will be in when you go to market. This is the time to start tightening up on unnecessary expenditures or over-generous salaries and benefits.

Establishing a medium-term business plan

A good medium-term business plan, carefully drawn up and thought out and put into action, will do much more than improve the operational effectiveness of the business. The challenge of originating the business plan in the first place will concentrate your mind on strengths, weaknesses, opportunities and threats and will force you to address all the options in a clear, forthright manner.

The plan itself will indicate your aspirations in terms of turnover, margins, profits and net assets, and will, if updated regularly, engender considerable confidence in the mind of a prospective buyer. He will be more prepared to accept future projections when he can examine the record of achievements to date and observe corrective action being taken on an ongoing basis. He will welcome signs that the management team and indeed other employees are participating in a plan to improve and develop the business, building essential strengths for the future. Where these people are financially tied into the performance of the business, so much the better.

A benefit of this plan is the deliberate focus on areas of potential, helping the business to position itself in the right sectors.

Since the optimum price will probably be secured through an earnout formula, tied, that is, to future profits, the task of drawing up a suitable formula will be considerably simplified if a credible business plan is already in place.

However, a note of caution. You must ensure that this business plan is realistic and achievable. Since deferred earnout formulae are often built up on the basis of future projections, a badly drawn up or totally 'blue sky' plan can rebound on the seller with a vengeance.

Specific suggestions to improve the value of your business

1. Eliminate all unnecessary expenditure or over-generous benefits to family and dependants, with the objective of minimising adjustments that the buyer must make to reported profits to calculate *real* profits. If your dependants urgently need money on an ongoing basis, pass it to them via dividends. This will be regarded as a *distribution* of profit, not a cost.

2. One objective of the business plan should be to smooth turnover and profit improvement to achieve a predictable growth trajectory. If stock or work in progress has been undervalued in the past, you should now aim to bring it on to a prudent but realistic basis over the next two or three years.

3. If you have surplus assets in the business, or assets that are not fully used, take appropriate action now. Why permit a buyer to realise these windfall profits?

4. Clear the decks of problems, such as doubtful debts, unrealistic depreciation rates, outstanding litigation, unrecognised losses etc. It is better to 'take a hit' on these in the first year of your business plan, giving the business time for the essential qualities to show through.

5. Invest in management (even at some cost to your bottom line) in the early years. Your aim should be to work yourself out of a job – to become a non-executive chairman, ideally – by training others to take over most of your functions and decision making.

   You must insist that your managers, in turn, groom other employees to cover for them. A clear succession line in the company with well-trained, flexible employees is a significant advantage to offer a purchaser.

6. If the company has unrelated side activities that you wish to retain personally after a sale, spin these off into separate subsidiaries as soon as possible. Equally, if you are putting some of the company's turnover through other businesses when it really forms an integral part of the operation to be sold, now is the time to stream these sales and profits through the main company.

7. Take another look at freehold property. We have discussed this earlier. Now is the time to regularise the situation here, one way or the other.

   Often property dealing distorts the results of the basic business and can reduce the apparent profitability, making it difficult for a buyer to see the wood for the trees.

   It is almost always better to present a clean trading company to potential buyers rather than force them to make conservative assumptions on carrying costs or resale values.

   If this is your situation, or if you intend to hold on to the freehold property post-sale, put it into a separate subsidiary and, ideally, charge an arm's-length rent to the trading company to be sold. But seek good tax advice first.

8. In drawing up a business plan for future operations, you would certainly look at the image and reputation that the company projects to the outside world.

   Consider the appearance of the offices, particularly the reception area. The design of your stationery and letter-

heading, brochures, advertising material, product literature and articles written about the company, are all
worthy of examination. Now is a good time to update and
modernise them, making sure that they project a con-
sistent and forward-looking image of the business.

I am not suggesting for one moment that you are going
to spend £20–£30 million on a new logo or company
colour scheme. Not all of us have the resources of a Pru-
dential Assurance or British Telecom to contemplate
such expenditure.

However, for relatively small sums the company's
image can often be considerably improved. This should,
in any event, result in additional interest and will
certainly be instrumental in creating the right first impression to a potential buyer. Remember, first impressions
die hard.

9. Take another look at long-term contracts. Where the
   timing is propitious, maybe you should renegotiate the
   terms or extend these contracts if favourable to you.
   Where a particular contract could prove expensive,
   consider ways of minimising or containing that risk. Tie in
   key employees, if possible, with contracts providing substantial performance incentives.

10. Ask your accountants or financial advisers to re-examine
    accounting policies and suggest any improvements. You
    should project the company as operating prudently and
    with stable, if progressive, policies.

11. Hold back on your own and your families' drawings from
    the business. Try to draw salary and benefits com-
    mensurate with those that an arm's-length manager or
    executive would expect. Remember that any additional
    annual profits accepted by a buyer may easily be subject
    to a *five or six times* multiple in terms of the eventual
    purchase price achieved.

12. Look at the company's liquidity. A company with good
    working capital is obviously easier to sell than a company
    struggling under a mountain of short-term debt. You
    certainly don't want the company to get into liquidity
    problems when you are trying to engineer a sale. This can
    easily put pressure on existing shareholders, clouding

their judgement and inclining them to accept quick and less than optimum deals.

13. In terms of credit facilities, lock in adequate finance if possible on a medium- to long-term basis. To have the company's very existence dependent on lending facilities which are virtually repayable on demand is not going to help you achieve the best price. All other things being equal, a buyer will prefer a company with liabilities in the form of trade creditors and term loans rather than bank overdrafts.

14. If shareholders have lent money to the company in the past, consider converting this into equity as part of a programme to tidy up the balance sheet. It will be regarded as equity in effect by a buyer in any case.

15. Get up-to-date valuations of the principal assets and update them regularly. Where unrealised profits are substantial, a case can be made for recognising such increases in the balance sheet and showing the surplus as a capital reserve.

16. Consider using retained earnings to declare dividends. This can be a tax-effective manoeuvre. Of course, professional tax advice is essential.

17. While striving to improve profits do not skimp on sensible product development. The buyer must be allowed to rationalise the price he is paying by being able to visualise a range of attractive new products coming on-stream.

Conclusion

You can now appreciate that improving the value of the business goes way beyond merely improving its current performance in terms of profits, return on investment and so on. This would certainly help you to get a better price when it is time to sell, but this is only part of the picture.

However, I am not recommending simply cosmetic changes, although better presentation of the company's market position, performance and profits is vital. Let us not forget that your objective is to end on a high note, not go out with a whimper.

Your target must be to develop a business with good product potential and sell this company into a rising market, ideally where confidence in the general economic future of both the industry and the country is high. In addition, it is not enough to put together a business plan designed to enhance the value of your company; it is vital to translate this plan into positive action.

If you have any doubts about your ability to design and follow through such a plan, seek outside help. There are many consultants in the UK who will help you to improve the business. There are not so many who could put together a good business plan designed to improve both the profits of the business and also its eventual value. There are even fewer who can do this *and* are also willing to work with you over the longer term to ensure that the target benefits are, in fact, achieved.

If you are serious about getting the best price for your business in a few years' time, fees incurred on such a consultant, typically on the basis of one or two days a quarter, should be handsomely rewarded when you do finally sell.

Chapter 16

Choosing an Adviser

Growth of business activity

The 1980s saw a veritable explosion of business activity, particularly at the small end of the market. There seem to be more entrepreneurs around than ever and many small companies were established in the boom years of the Thatcher government.

This trend has been strongly encouraged by both the government and the clearing banks, as their literature will demonstrate, and the number of new company formations has been at a record high.

There have, of course, been a lot of failures. Equally, however, there have been many companies that have done well and grown into substantial organisations or have been taken over by larger companies. The scene is one of constant evolution whereby entrepreneurs start small, sell out to larger groups and reinvest the proceeds in a new business venture.

It is an open and competitive market in the UK but there tend to be fewer family companies today than in previous generations.

Sources of advice

The large end of this market is well served: the quoted public companies and the larger private companies have been historically well catered for by merchant banks in the City of London. Here we are talking of companies with a value of, perhaps, £15–£20 million or more. This has always been a fairly active sector and one that is well publicised in the press.

At the small end of the market, where we are talking about retail shops, small manufacturing, distribution or other service businesses worth, perhaps, anything from £50,000 to £200,000, owners have historically been served by brokers. The tribal notice-board is probably *Dalton's Weekly* (no relation of mine!) and the business brokers essentially offer an informal introduction service leaving the negotiations to the principals involved.

Brokers typically list opportunities on investment registers and rely on the sheer volume of introductions to create transactions and, of course, fees for themselves. Some specialise. The Christie Group plc (not the auctioneers) is active in the hotel, public house and restaurant sector. Diverco, a company based in Worcester, has represented small sellers for many years.

Essentially though, in this sector, it is a case of *caveat emptor* – let the buyer beware – since most of the 'digging' or investigation work has to be done by the buyer.

This book is particularly addressed to medium-sized companies falling between the two extremes cited above. In this case, we are talking of companies with a value of between £500,000 and perhaps £15 million. The traditional advisers in this sector have been accountants, solicitors and bankers – old family advisers who have sometimes known the company owners for many years both professionally and socially.

Traditional advisers

However, with increasing activity and competition the scene is changing. For a variety of reasons, the ability of such traditional advisers to offer suitable services is no longer unquestioned, and the range of services required by the vendors themselves is changing significantly in an increasingly competitive market place.

The accountant has long been the favoured traditional adviser and is still involved in most medium-sized transactions: advising vendors, corresponding with the buyer's accountants and responding to their requirements for additional information regarding his client's business.

However, local firms of accountants are finding the demands imposed on them by their clients, professional associations, taxation and various regulatory authorities are becoming more and more demanding. They have to be careful when giving financial advice and may well feel that they have their hands full advising on the accounting and tax ramifications of proposed deals.

The typical local firm tends to be relatively small and, of necessity, able to offer only a limited range of skills. There is also inevitably a possible conflict of interest. A successful transaction often means a lost audit client.

The banker, another traditional adviser in past years, was seen as a well-established, reputable member of local society. Frequently, he served as branch manager for 10 or 15 years, which meant that he came to know his customers very well. He also knew many businessmen through membership of Round Table, Rotary or local golf clubs.

As we have commented before, however, the role of the bank manager is also changing dramatically and, in many cases, two or three years at one branch is about the maximum time to be spent there now. There is tremendous pressure on the banks to produce profits at branch level and the local manager is becoming more of an administrator than a general business confidant to his major customers.

To counteract this, the banks are setting up small business advisory centres but this tends to be a rather different animal – more interested, in my experience, in pensions, mortgages and insurance.

The third traditional adviser is the solicitor who, like the accountant, is under considerable competitive pressure, particularly since fees derived from property conveyancing are much more difficult to come by. The solicitor is finding it difficult to maintain his role as the local 'philosopher' although he will inevitably be involved in documenting any transaction in its later stages.

The vendor's requirements are also changing. Since the buyer is increasingly likely to be a national or even international organisation rather than a local businessman, the vendor needs negotiation skills of a different order. The vendor himself may no longer be the archetypal family man retiring at 65, but is quite likely to be a young, thrusting entrepreneur of 40-something who has decided to sell his current business and reinvest the proceeds in a more congenial lifestyle or a brand new career. Such a vendor will have difficulty relating satisfactorily to the traditional advisers and will be impatient for action.

Acquisition and divestment consultants

As a response to these changing circumstances, new organisations are emerging, designed specifically to help the medium-sized business vendor.

Some of the merchant banks, for instance, having identified a new niche market, have decided to offer merger and acquisition services to such businessmen. A few have made a genuine strategic commitment to the sector and offer a professional and supportive service.

Other merchant banks, in the light of the current difficult economic situation and the lack of bigger deals, have reluctantly 'descended' into this sector. Their services tend to be much more impersonal, cavalier and ineffectual.

A number of the national and international firms of chartered accountants have established merger and acquisition departments or divisions. This move was designed primarily to provide a broader range of services to their own clients, and when handling a sale they will inevitably look through their own client list first. An investment register will be used to deal with the 'difficult to place' situations where they are reluctant to commit much time and effort.

At the time of writing, most of the merger and acquisition departments of the chartered accountancy firms are thin on the ground, their more capable professionals having been seconded to the receivership department in response to frantic requests for more manpower.

There are one or two law firms offering merger and acquisition services but with predictable emphasis on the legal aspects and advice on the transaction.

A few consulting firms dedicated to merger and acquisition work have emerged recently. Most were set up in the halcyon days of the late 1980s and are currently experiencing their first real market down-turn. Others were established in the

1970s and are more familiar with changing business cycles and
the inherent volatility in this field.

Business brokers

Before turning to the choice of an adviser, we should perhaps
say a few words about business brokers, those hardy peren-
nials who will undertake to sell your business on a purely con-
tingency-fee basis. In other words, if your business does not
sell no fee is payable.

The typical broker is constantly on the move and you can
catch him on his car phone if you have the number. Calls to his
office will elicit a 'canned' response from a telephone
answering machine and if do you speak to him in person it is
likely to be at 7 o'clock in the evening. His other key piece of
equipment is a fast photocopying machine.

His forte is signing up lots of potential deals, scattering the
information as widely as possible in the expectation and
indeed realistic anticipation that some transactions will result
from minimum efforts on his part. Throw lots of mud at the
wall. Some will stick!

A cautionary tale drawn from our own experience will help
you to understand the way in which the broker operates.

In London there is one well-known professional running a
company brokering service primarily through the circulation,
far and wide, of an investment opportunity register. He
assures the vendor that there are no charges since all fees are
paid by the buyer. It is a service that promises swift and
effective results and is often preceded by a good evening's
entertainment 'on the town', during which the broker
describes the range of his services to the vendor. Over the
port, you conclude that this broker must be doing half the
deals in London and you are fortunate that he is prepared to
take you on.

A large foreign-owned group fell for this line and
authorised the broker to sell a subsidiary which it had been
decided to divest. The hard-nosed chief executive officer in
the UK sensed that here was value for money and was
agreeably surprised to be presented with a tight timetable for

completion of the transaction. He was assured that everything would be kept totally confidential and that his firm's role in negotiating and completing the transaction would be minimal.

Having secured the mandate, the broker listed the opportunity on his investment register in attractive detail – it was obviously an ideal situation for a thrusting entrepreneur (ideal starter home?). The flood of enquirers were required to sign an impressive confidentiality agreement which also included, however, an undertaking to pay the broker's full fees. These undertakings can be onerous and can create sweeping liabilities on the part of the buyer. Only the most blasé buyers will consider signing such a document without first taking legal advice.

In such circumstances, is it surprising that the potential buyer is cavalier also with regard to the confidentiality of the information provided? In return for a signature on this agreement the broker identifies the company and provides brief details of the business together with the latest available audited accounts. To some buyers this amounts to being granted a hunting licence.

You may be able to forecast the results. In many cases, the seller is swamped with enquiries, telephone calls and approaches and some buyers will even turn up unannounced demanding to be taken around and shown the business. After all, they have signed a full confidentiality agreement. They will often treat this as a licence to tramp over everyone and everything and ask any questions they deem relevant.

The broker is not unduly worried about the loss of confidentiality. His first allegiance, in any case, is to the deal and, of course, to his fee. His second allegiance is to the buyer who will pay his fee. The vendor, in consequence, is a long way down the field.

The broker wants to do a deal and the more difficult it becomes for the vendor to withdraw the better he likes it. He relies on customers, suppliers, competitors and even employees of the company to make sure that deal momentum is maintained.

Furthermore, the vendor has to do all the work and respond to all the questions. In many cases, vendors will be doing this directly with potential buyers since the broker has already moved on to the next deal. He figures that your deal is effectively 'in the bag'. He knows that his business is a volume business – win some, lose some!

Occasionally, half way through such an exercise the seller will come to us in despair asking for assistance, but at that point there is little we can do to help.

Making your choice

The first golden rule is to know and evaluate your own strengths, skills and resources and to decide what help you need. You may already have effectively delegated the day-to-day running of the company and can spend all your time negotiating a sale. Alternatively, you may still have a key role in the running of the business and will understandably not want to see this role suffer while you involve yourself in lengthy negotiations.

You may already have reached an informal agreement with, say, a trade buyer and simply require the services of an adviser to help you negotiate the best possible deal in the circumstances.

Alternatively, you may have narrowed your search for a buyer to a list of half a dozen or so, and want an adviser to contact these companies confidentially to determine which might make the best partner.

On the other hand, you may be starting with a clean slate and require a full service from your advisers, including the drawing up of a detailed sales memorandum describing the business, the identification of a range of suitable buyers to target and confidential contact with these buyers to determine which would welcome an approach.

Whatever decision you make, do not underestimate the time involved. Typically the process will take from six to nine months and may well involve detailed negotiations with at least two or three potential purchasers. It will require a high energy level and considerable patience on your part. Even if you do hire consultants for the full process you will still be very much one of the team, being required to work with them throughout the process.

If doing it yourself, you must ask yourself whether you have the skills to negotiate effectively with the buyer, bearing in mind that you may be asked to retain an ongoing role in the company for two to three years. Relationships fatally damaged during a hard negotiation process may not form the ideal start for a post-acquisition involvement.

Then there is the question of achieving an acceptable price. Having read the book this far you should have more realistic price expectations and may be able to form some judgement about the ease with which this price could be achieved. If your price expectation is ambitious, given all the circumstances, you would be well advised to appoint merger and acquisition consultants to help you. They will repay their fees many times over if they succeed in finding the right buyer for you.

Questions to ask

I suggest that as a first step you meet two or three specialist firms and discuss the type of service you require in confidence. Ask how they would approach the project and enquire whether or not it is of potential interest and appeal to them. Listen to the description of the services offered and ask them to put their recommendations to you in writing, together with brochures and background information on their organisation and its services.

In choosing a particular adviser bear the following points in mind:

Personal chemistry. How well did you get on with the people you met? Do they talk your language? Do they seem realistic? Do they have a reasonable background in and knowledge of your industry?
If you are in a narrow commercial sector, it may prove impossible to find someone with specific expertise in that area. Even if you did locate such an adviser he might well search too narrowly for a buyer and so could be unsuccessful. However, where you are operating in, say, the food or engineering sectors, you need to work with a specialist who is familiar with the terminology, processes, companies and personalities.

Who will carry out the assignment? Are you talking to the consultant who will be primarily responsible or is he really a business development officer? Is he in essence a one-man-band or will he work as part of a team to make sure that your objectives are met?
Bearing in mind that the process may take six to nine months it is essential to have continuity, and the skills required in understanding the business and identifying suitable buyers in the early stages of the assignment may differ from the skills required in negotiating an acceptable transaction later on. Hence the need for a team approach.

Does the firm have the resources to handle the assignment, particularly in the area of research and contacts?

Do you feel that the firm is prepared to spend time to get to know the company and understand its technology and potential? Does the adviser seem interested in identifying your own personal objectives?
Gauge the impact the firm is likely to have on potential buyers.

Has the firm mentioned your role in the process?
Needless to say, any mention of 'investment opportunity registers' at this stage should raise a red flag immediately in your mind.

Confidentiality. Will the firm handle the question of confidentiality with care and due respect to your own personal position?
If the attitude is in any way cavalier this will cause trouble during the project.

If a search is required, does the firm have access to a suitable range of databases, industry contacts etc? Does it favour a shotgun approach to identify buyers or prefer to pinpoint suitable targets one by one? What are the chances of identifying a 'jigsaw player' for your company?

Where the people you meet are part of a larger firm, is there any possible conflict of interest with their other activities or

client base? Do you suspect that, in reality, they will limit their search for a buyer to their current client list?

Are they proposing to report regularly to you on progress and are they able to suggest tentative time-scales for the completion of the transaction?

What do they think is the likelihood of a successful outcome of the engagement given the range of values you have indicated that you wish to achieve, together with any other conditions important to you?
One of the first questions that should arise in the preliminary interview is that of your price expectations. Any consultant taking on such an assignment without satisfying himself as to the reasonableness of your personal expectations and requirements is certainly not adopting a professional approach.

I recommend that you engage one firm to carry out a valuation as an initial step and agree to pay a reasonable fee for this service. This valuation can be done on the basis that if you go ahead and retain that firm, the cost of the valuation will be offset against future fees.

By having a written and detailed valuation carried out, you will gain a good insight into the firm's method of operation and the thoroughness with which the assignment is approached. Assuming the firm goes on to handle the full project, it will also give a head start when drawing up the sales memorandum. Bearing in mind also the firm's anticipation of being asked to sell the company, this should provide a strong incentive to come up with a realistic price. It is certainly not unknown, however, for consultants and, of course, estate agents to give a high initial valuation to try to secure the mandate.

Costs

No final choice of advisers can be made, of course, without reference to their charges both in terms of fees and the expenses they are likely to incur on your behalf.

Accountants and lawyers normally prefer to agree an hourly or daily rate with you for this work. With such an agreement there is no risk to them since their time is fully covered but, of course, there can be no guarantee that their efforts will be successful. All the risks in such a situation will be on your shoulders.

Such an approach may well be appropriate where you are using advisers in a specific role, such as negotiating a deal with a buyer that you have already identified or requesting specific research to uncover a suitable list of target buyers.

However, buying services on an hourly basis could be expensive. A full assignment normally involves the consultants in familiarising themselves with the company through visits, discussions etc, preparing sales memoranda, carrying out market research to identify suitable buyers, contacting a whole range of potential buyers and bringing a specific buyer to the negotiating table, leading up to the preparation of a detailed letter of intent.

Typically, such an assignment will take anything from 300 to 500 hundred hours of work on behalf of the principals and you do not need a calculator to work out that at £120–£140 an hour this could be quite a sizeable fee, without any guarantee that the final result will be acceptable to you.

Because of the inherent risk element in such an assignment, most merger and acquisition consultants will work on a part-contingent basis, ie they will look for an initial upfront deposit or commitment fee on account of their services but will anticipate receiving their full fee only on the successful completion of a transaction.

Mention will probably be made of the Lehman Scale which is the traditional US fee scale for merger and acquisition transactions. This scale has been adopted, more or less intact, by UK merger and acquisition specialists. The fee is based on the total consideration passing, very broadly defined incidentally, and is calculated as follows:

On the first $1 million or, say, £500,000 of consideration
5% or £25,000

On the next $1 million or, say, £500,000 of consideration
4% or £20,000

On the next $1 million or, say, £500,000 of consideration
3% or £15,000

On the next $1 million or, say, £500,000 of consideration
2% or £10,000

On any excess   1% or £10,000

You can see, therefore, that a £2 million transaction would generate a total fee to the adviser of £70,000. He would look for 1 per cent on any consideration in excess of £2 million.

Most firms will insist on a commitment fee at the start of the project of anything from £75000 to £25,000 which will be deductible from the final success fee. They will also require that out-of-pocket costs be invoiced and reimbursed monthly. In this case, it is important that you define with them what constitutes acceptable out-of-pocket costs and you should ask for an estimate of their likely monthly charges. The consultant should agree to clear in advance with you any significant out-of-pocket costs such as expenses incurred in advertising, extensive research or overseas travel undertaken as part of the project.

Normally you will be asked to sign terms and conditions incorporating the above charges and you should not hesitate to query any clauses in the agreement that you do not fully understand.

Conclusion

As the vendor, only you can decide the level of advice you need to help sell your company. It is certainly a much more complicated exercise than selling a house and most people do not hesitate to engage an estate agent for that purpose.

Never underestimate the amount of work involved or the time required to complete this exercise and before undertaking it yourself be sure that you have the experience required, the emotional stamina and the time available.

Appendix: Valuation Checklist

Preliminary basic information

Can a valuation be made of my type of company
using conventional yardsticks? (Chapter 9)   Yes/No

Are there *any* complications which would affect the
saleability or value of my business? (Chapter 12)   Yes/No

Am I prepared to be flexible in terms of timing,
form of consideration and post-sale involvement?
(Chapter 13)   Yes/No

Do I have a particular date in mind at which to
make a valuation?   Yes/No

Background financial information

Do I have the basic information needed?
- Audited accounts for the last four years?   Yes/No
- Current and next year's projected results?   Yes/No
- Record of adjustments and exceptional items?   Yes/No
- Current freehold, leasehold, equipment and
  rental valuations?   Yes/No
- Surveys, forecasts, broker comment on my
  market sector?   Yes/No
- Sufficient background on recent comparable
  transactions?   Yes/No

Calculate a valuation on earnings

Can I calculate maintainable profits? (Chapter 6)   Yes/No

– Develop maintainable earnings
– Summarise real profits and examine trends.

Can I decide profit multiples?   Yes/No

– Calculate a reasonable discount to be applied?.   ☐
– Is there an applicable sector – if not, can I
  identify likely quoted buyers?   Yes/No
– Develop average price/earnings multiple?   ☐

Calculate an earnings-based valuation,
multiplying maintainable earnings by P/E
multiple?   ☐

Calculate the value of tangible assets (Chapter 7)

Summarise asset values from audited accounts.   ☐
Adjust to current value for property, stock,
debtors etc.   ☐
Adjust, if necessary, for net trading results to
date.   ☐
Consider quality/realisability of assets.   ☐
Adopt an asset value.   ☐

Consider intangible values (Chapter 8)

– Are there any services, products, positioning,
  potential, reputation, nuisance value etc which
  sets my company apart from its competitors?
  Synergy?   Yes/No
– Would a buyer pay a premium to take over (or
  eliminate) a competitor?   Yes/No
– Can I estimate a value to the buyer?   Yes/No

The economic background (Chapter 10)

- Consider the market sector, financial position
  and outlook of probable trade buyers. ☐
- Consider market sentiment and interest rate
  levels. ☐
- Consider recent transactions. Are they helpful? Yes/No

Other complications (Chapter 12)

- Are there *any* other factors or complications
  which will affect value? ☐

Pulling it together (Chapter 11)

Can I draw a 'snake' based on information/facts
developed?   Yes/No
Can I make a crude check of this value for:

- Goodwill?   Yes/No
- hurdle rates?   Yes/No

Is this valuation sufficient for my present
purposes?   Yes/No
If not, might a more accurate valuation affect my
future course of action?   Yes/No

Glossary

Add-backs   These are adjustments made to the reported or audited profits of the business to account for both extraordinary or exceptional profits and losses and also for expenses, benefits, perquisites taken out of the business by a private owner which would not normally be payable by a company run totally at arm's length. Unless charges on the business are wholly, exclusively and necessarily incurred to promote that business, they should be added back.

Adjusted earnings   The actual performance that would be expected of a business operating independently, ie not relying on parent or group services, benefits or concessions and equally freed up from parent/group charges or management fees not based on objective or arm's-length costs.

Alpha shares or stocks   About 150 of the most actively traded and important shares on the Stock Exchange. Beta, Gamma and Delta are progressively less important quoted companies.

Annual maintainable earnings   The calculation of a conservative level of earnings, pre-tax, that a business can reasonably be expected to maintain over the next few years. These earnings will have been adjusted for perquisites and benefits paid to owners in excess of arm's-length management remuneration due to them based on the value of actual services rendered.

Asset cover   The extent to which the consideration or purchase price paid is represented by tangible and realisable assets. This is one indication of the investment risk faced. If the worst comes to the worst the assets presumably can be sold and a large proportion of the purchase price recovered.

Base line valuation The most conventional method of valuing your business to produce an immediate cash value can be regarded as a base line valuation. This can be used as a yardstick against which other valuations involving differing forms of consideration, timing, conditions etc can be compared.

Blue chip The highest quality investment available. An investment which should be worry-free and non-speculative.

Bolt-on acquisition An acquisition that the buying company finds easy to assimilate or 'bolt on' to its existing operations.

Business Expansion Scheme (BES) A government-sponsored scheme designed to encourage personal taxpayers to invest as sleeping or non-active investors in private companies. The scheme is designed to help smaller businesses raise capital and an annual investment of up to £40,000 is deductible from the investor's taxable income. For the investment to be eligible for tax relief, BES criteria must be met and Inland Revenue approval secured beforehand. Capital gains on the proceeds of sale of the shares are tax free provided the investment is kept for a minimum of five years. To be discontinued from 31 December 1993.

Buyout An agreed amount of deferred consideration taken as part of a sale transaction. This may be guaranteed by the company or by a bank and may be dependent on terms and conditions agreed between the parties (note that a 'management buyout' is something quite different).

Cluster effect Where valuations are built up on different bases using varying formulae and are plotted graphically, we search for a cluster effect of the points plotted. Such a cluster gives us an indication of the range of values to be expected for that business and engenders a higher degree of confidence in the final valuation adopted.

Consideration A somewhat technical word for the amount paid for the purchase of a business. Consideration is a broad term and can include either immediate or deferred cash and all other benefits in kind such as pension contributions, consulting fees, forgiveness of loans, assuming liabilities including personal guarantees on bank overdrafts etc.

Convertible loan note   A convertible loan note is frequently issued by the purchaser of a business as part of the consideration paid to the seller. This acknowledgement of a debt or IOU is convertible into cash by the seller at a future date and may or may not bear interest. The debt may be secured on the assets of the business or guaranteed by the purchaser or, better, by a bank. In addition to minimising the cash outlay required of the purchaser, a loan note may enable the vendor to defer capital gains tax payable on the sale.

Covenant   An undertaking given in respect of borrowings to abide by conditions, ratios etc imposed by the lender. Serious failure to observe such covenants can 'trigger' an act of default which may give the lender the right to demand immediate repayment of the loan in full. Covenants are also used in connection with leases.

Declining balance basis of depreciation   One basic method of providing for depreciation whereby depreciation is calculated on a declining balance each period. Under this method the asset is never completely written off and for an equal percentage rate it provides a slower rate of write off than straight line depreciation.

Directors' depredations   This is another phrase to describe the full range of benefits extracted by the owners and directors of a private business not wholly and necessarily incurred for the profitable conduct of that business.

Discount back   Expressing the value of future benefits in present cash terms by applying a 'negative' interest rate or discount factor. This rate should be appropriate for the term envisaged.

Discounted cash flow   A method of calculating the present cash value of a stream of future cash receipts and payments to be derived from a business investment. The future cash movements must be determinable with some confidence both as to amount and timing. Current interest rates for the period envisaged and appropriate to the perceived risks involved must also be assumed. This can be an effective method of assessing the relative financial attractiveness of two or three competing projects. This method is, however, totally inappropriate for high-risk uncertain projects or profit streams.

Discounting the sector multiple   The owner of a private business cannot normally expect to get the same value for his shares, relative to earnings, as an investor would pay for shares in a similar, publicly quoted company. A reduction or discount in the price/earnings multiple will be applied to reflect the lack of liquidity offered in private company shares and to compensate for perceived increased risks in the investment etc.

Distractive index   This expression describes an owner trying to fill, simultaneously, two conflicting roles: acting as managing director to run a business in the most efficient and profitable manner, while at the same time developing and carrying out a protracted campaign to find a buyer for the company. All too often the results are disastrous.

'Double whammy'   Colloquially known as having your cake and eating it too. An example would be accepting deferred consideration, based on post-acquisition profit performance, which can be taken either in cash or in shares at an advantageous or predetermined price based on current share values. If your company is substantial, in relation to the quoted plc buying, you may benefit twice – once based on profits you have actually generated and again as a result of those profits boosting the plc's performance and future share price.

Another similar expression, 'double dipping', refers to a company's ability to take two lots of capital allowances on the same assets using differing tax regimes.

Earn out   Deferred consideration, taken as part of a sale transaction, which is dependent on and calculated by reference to future performance of the business acquired.

Fallback bid During a programme to sell your business it is likely that an interested buyer will put forward an opening bid or sighting shot. He may not seriously believe that this offer will be accepted but will hope that it will reveal more clearly your price expectations. Such an offer is psychologically useful to have in hand when talking to other interested buyers. In many cases it engenders a sense of confidence on the part of the seller which transmits quickly to buyers with whom he is in contact.

Float of shares In connection with a public company, this refers to the percentage of the total issued shares in the hands of the general public rather than locked away by significant long-term shareholders such as directors, institutions, pension funds etc.

Freezer trust A trust established to receive assets, including shares, enabling capital gains tax payable on disposal of assets to be deferred, or frozen, until some future date. In certain circumstances tax can be avoided completely.

Gilts These are government bonds or gilt edged securities and offer high security of income and capital, although the market value will tend to rise and fall according to prevailing interest rates. The return on gilts provides a useful bench mark or standard for what interest is available on essentially a passive non-risk investment. When investing in a risk situation, such as a private business, the investor will obviously demand a higher rate of return to compensate for the additional risk.

Goodwill While accountants may place differing formal interpretations on 'goodwill', for our purposes goodwill can be defined as that part of the purchase price not represented by the book value of net assets acquired.

Hard liabilities Those liabilities which are contractual, defined, real and all too quantifiable. The creditor may have little difficulty in measuring and enforcing his claim and may go to law to do so.

Hurdle rate   The annual rate of return that a potential new investment must yield to justify serious consideration by the investor. This rate will be influenced by prevailing interest rates and borrowing costs and also by the availability of alternative investment opportunities.

Indexation   With respect to capital gains tax, the Inland Revenue do not seek to impose tax on purely inflationary gains – gains reflecting in effect the declining purchasing value of the pound. For this purpose, the Revenue supply indexation tables indicating the cumulative impact of inflation on a monthly basis since March 1982 – the last base date for valuation of assets. Only gains realised exceeding the indexed value are taxable. Generally, gains made prior to March 1982 are no longer considered taxable.

Investment opportunity register   This is a register maintained by a merger broker which provides summary information on business investment opportunities available. It may also include details of buyers' requirements. The broker should be able to provide a 'taster' to all enquirers and a full selling memorandum to serious potential purchasers under suitable confidentiality undertakings.

Jigsaw player   A jigsaw player is a premium buyer who has identified your business as a missing piece in the jigsaw he is assembling. Your company may cover a geographic market in which he is not represented, produce goods which reflect a gap in his own product line, or provide access to markets for his range of products that he has been unable to penetrate.

Lehman scale   Merger and acquisition consultants and brokers are frequently remunerated on the basis of fees proportionate to the consideration passing or purchase price paid. For this purpose, a sliding fee scale, the Lehman Scale (after Lehman Brothers, a US investment bank), is often used.

This scale is as follows:

On the first $1,000,000 or, say, £500,000	5%
On the next $1,000,000 or, say, £500,000	4%
On the next $1,000,000 or, say, £500,000	3%
On the next $1,000,000 or, say, £500,000	2%
On consideration in excess of $4,000,000 or £2,000,000	1%

Letter of intent   This is a detailed and formal document signed by both buyer and seller defining the principal terms and conditions of an agreement to transfer ownership in a business. Unlike the actual sales contract, it may not be legally enforceable. It is designed to serve as a blueprint for lawyers and accountants and is also often called the 'Heads of Agreement'.

Management buy in (MBI)   The sale of a business to a new or outside management team, usually formed to participate in such an investment, is termed a management buy in. The investment will usually be supported by a financial institution – a leveraged buy in.

Management buy out (MBO)   The sale of a business to the *existing management*, who will usually be supported by a financial institution – a leveraged buy out.

Portfolio investor   One who makes a passive or non-active investment in a business. The objective might be income or capital growth, or indeed both, but he or she will not seek to become actively involved in running the business. The investor will view the profits as alternatives to income from 'gilts' or, say, property.

Predictable buyer   A predictable buyer is one who would normally be considered as part of a logical and professional research programme. He or she may be a competitor or someone who sells to or buys from the company. The formal valuation of a company should be based on the price that such a trade buyer would expect to pay.

Premium buyer   This is the ideal purchaser of your company, often a trade buyer who can recognise the underlying value of the company and its potential for expansion and development. Often he or she can identify the benefits to be gained by combining with your company to increase market penetration, reduce overhead etc. A buyer with such advantages can often afford to pay a much better price than other purchasers.

Price/earnings multiples and ratios   This is a multiple calculated by dividing the consideration or purchase price for the business by the adjusted annual maintainable profits. It can be expressed on either a pretax or post-tax basis. P/E multiples for public quoted companies are always given on a post-tax basis. However, with a private company a pretax multiple is in some ways more useful.

Price/volume trade offs   Conventional wisdom suggests that increasing the sales price of products or services will diminish demand but improve the gross margin on each unit sold. A well-run business will try to maximise total profit by getting this 'mix' of volume and price right, taking into account inherent constraints including market demand, equipment, personnel, finance etc.

Rollover relief   The sale of assets at a profit, in Inland Revenue terms, will normally give rise to capital gains tax on those profits. If the proceeds of sale are reinvested, within a reasonable period, into other 'qualifying' assets, the tax payer is able to 'roll over' or defer the capital gains tax payable until the new asset acquired is finally sold.

Sleeper   A business with a low profile in the industry – not well known or widely publicised. It might well occupy a profitable niche in the market place or have a product with considerable potential for profitable growth. The present owner may be satisfied with a modest rate of return and rely on personal referrals and established relationships to maintain business rather than actively promote the business through advertising, trade associations, etc. The business may not even have been incorporated as a limited company.

Soft assets   Assets which are an integral part of the ongoing business but are difficult to identify, measure or realise separately. In the event of a receivership or liquidation, these values may well quickly disappear. Goodwill is the classic example of a soft asset.

Sole trader   A business person trading in his or her own name assuming personal responsibility for liabilities incurred. Most business people will use the 'umbrella' of a limited company for this purpose, becoming a director of the company.

Two sole traders joining together become a partnership, another potentially cumbersome situation involving personal responsibility for partnership debts.

Straight line depreciation   Providing for depreciation on an asset by charging an equal amount each period, typically a year, until the asset is completely written off. A 10 per cent rate of depreciation on a £100,000 asset would imply charging depreciation of £10,000 per annum for ten years. Using a similar percentage on a declining balance basis the charge for the first year only would be similar; thereafter the amount charged would decline.

Super profits   Those profits a business is capable of producing over and above borrowing costs on the full investment.

Synergy   A buzz-word in boom times – accountants talk about two plus two making five! Basically, the additional values to be derived or created by putting two complementary businesses together. Value may be created, for example, by providing the sales force with additional products to sell or by eliminating excess overhead by combining two administrative systems. There is often significant scope for such savings *provided* that the buyers' management is tough-minded and determined.

Tangible assets   Assets of a business that can be identified, measured and quantified with some element of precision.

These typically include cash, deposits, debtors, motor vehicles, freehold property, plant and machinery, inventory etc. Some, such as plant and machinery, while tangible, may not be easily convertible into cash.

Taster   A brief one- or two-page description of a business for sale designed to help a potential buyer determine whether the opportunity might be of real interest or not. It will generally not identify the company but will highlight specific features of possible interest to buyers.

Tax shelter   An investment approved by the Inland Revenue, which enables the taxpayer to defer, or shelter, taxes which would otherwise be payable. Examples include investments in Business Expansion Schemes, qualifying industrial buildings, assets attracting capital allowances etc.

Vendor placing   A quoted public company may issue new shares in lieu of cash for part or whole of the consideration. Where the vendor is reluctant to accept such shares, it is sometimes possible to 'place' them with an institution, keen to increase its shareholding, who will purchase them from the vendor for cash. This is called a 'vendor placing'.

Washing its face   An industry expression which indicates that the cash flow obtainable from an acquisition will be sufficient to cover the interest and servicing costs of the investment, assuming that the purchase is 100 per cent funded through bank borrowings.

Index